Early Assistance from Potentially Responsible Parties After Human-Made Disasters

NICHOLAS M. PACE, LLOYD DIXON

RAND SOCIAL AND ECONOMIC WELL-BEING

For more information on this publication, visit www.rand.org/t/RR3022

Library of Congress Cataloging-in-Publication Data is available for this publication.
ISBN: 978-1-9774-0380-3

Published by the RAND Corporation, Santa Monica, Calif.

Preface

Providing assistance to individuals and businesses soon after a disaster can play an important role in reducing suffering and accelerating the community's return to something approaching normality. When the disaster is of anthropogenic origin, parties potentially responsible for the onset of the event can be an important source of early assistance—particularly when such assistance is offered long before the party is under any obligation to do so as the result of the settlement of tort claims or the judgment of a court of law. Besides providing relief to those adversely affected by the disaster, such assistance can reduce the delay and transaction costs associated with seeking compensation through the more traditional tort liability process.

The authors examine issues involved in the provision of early assistance by potentially responsible parties (PRPs). They provide examples of how early assistance has worked in practice and describe the benefits and drawbacks of early assistance from the perspectives of PRPs and their insurers, victims, and plaintiff lawyers. They also identify potential changes in sentencing guidelines, guidance for calculating sanctions and punitive damages, and compensation frameworks that could encourage PRPs to provide early assistance. Policymakers might consider such measures should they determine that the benefits of encouraging early assistance outweigh possible reductions in the degree to which socially undesirable behaviors are deterred.

Justice Policy Program

RAND Social and Economic Well-Being is a division of the RAND Corporation that seeks to actively improve the health and social and economic well-being of populations and communities throughout the world. This research was conducted in the Justice Policy Program within RAND Social and Economic Well-Being. The program focuses on such topics as access to justice, policing, corrections, drug policy, and court system reform, as well as other policy concerns pertaining to public safety and criminal and civil justice. For more information, email justicepolicy@rand.org.

RAND Ventures

The RAND Corporation is a research organization that develops solutions to public policy challenges to help make communities throughout the world safer and more secure, healthier, and more prosperous. RAND is nonprofit, nonpartisan, and committed to the public interest.

RAND Ventures is a vehicle for investing in policy solutions. Philanthropic contributions support our ability to take the long view, tackle tough and often-controversial topics, and share our findings in innovative and compelling ways. RAND's research findings and recommendations are based on data and evidence, and therefore do not necessarily reflect the policy preferences or interests of its clients, donors, or supporters.

Funding for this venture was provided by gifts from RAND supporters and income from operations.

Contents

Tables

Summary

In the immediate aftermath of a disaster, first responders, charitable aid organizations, and community members perform invaluable services for society by stabilizing dangerous situations and preventing further personal injury, loss of life, and property damage. But when the disaster may have had an anthropogenic origin, the U.S. system of tort liability can also play a role in the recovery process. Those impacted adversely by the event may seek to recover their losses from the alleged potentially responsible parties (PRPs), advancing demands for compensation or other relief, either directly—from those believed to be responsible—or indirectly, from the third-party liability insurers of those parties. Typically, the process is lengthy, given the generally adversarial relationship between the disaster's victims and those believed to be at fault. Often, the possibility of protracted and costly litigation leads entities that appear and to have contributed to the onset of the event to take a defensive stance and to refrain from taking any action at all, in fear it might create even the appearance of accepting legal fault.

In many instances, however, PRPs at risk of being immersed in a flurry of lawsuits in the weeks and months after the disaster unfolded will, nevertheless, engage in an aggressive program that offers assistance to individuals, businesses, and local governments that have incurred losses. This assistance, sometimes first offered within hours of the start of the incident, can range from handing out hotel vouchers to evacuees to setting up sophisticated programs that facilitate the processing of claims for property damage, business disruption, medical expenses, and other losses. We describe such aid as a form of "assistance" rather than "compensation" because the signature feature of compensation as a form of *quid pro quo*, in which money is given in exchange for releasing a party from potential tort liability, may not always be present. An offer of assistance might, for example, have no purpose other than to ameliorate the suffering of others. We also characterize this assistance as being "early" in its timing, as it is provided (or at least offered) relatively soon after the onset of the event and long before the business is obligated to make such provision, either as the result of the settlement of tort claims or the judgment of a court of law. Such early assistance can sometimes fill gaps in the overall disaster response that are not always addressed by other resources such as nongovernmental organizations and first responders.

This paper describes illustrative instances where early assistance was offered, explores the benefits and drawbacks of early assistance from the perspective of different stakeholders, and examines potential options for encouraging PRPs to provide early assistance should policymakers decide that it is desirable to do so. Our goals for this paper were limited to describing how early assistance occurred in four admittedly unique instances and how some possible changes in the substantive and procedural law might incentivize PRPs to take a more active role. The paper is not meant to address fundamental issues in disaster-response policy, suggest that PRPs can always be more effective in the post-disaster context than traditional responders such as the Red Cross or the Federal Emergency Management Agency (FEMA), or advocate for the implementation of any of the potential legal changes.

Research Questions and Methods

Our interest in early assistance arises from its potential to speed recovery, reduce the overall losses caused by an event, and reduce litigation and related transaction costs. To this end, this study addresses three main questions.

1. What are examples of how early assistance has played out in practice?

2. What are the perceived benefits and drawbacks of early assistance from the viewpoints of different stakeholders, including victims, PRPs, insurers, and counsel?
3. If early assistance is deemed useful, what are various options for encouraging PRPs to provide early assistance?

We initially reviewed controlling legal authority with a focus on the evidentiary implications of PRP actions in any assessment of liability following an adverse event. Secondary legal literature (law review articles, legal treatises, etc.), legal periodicals, and topical guides were searched as well.

We also conducted a series of semistructured, not-for-attribution interviews with outside counsel for corporations that had been PRPs in the past, in-house counsel for similar entities, plaintiffs' attorneys, special masters, academics, and insurers. The interviewees were purposely selected to reflect a broad range of stakeholder and expert groups, and we targeted candidates who were knowledgeable about issues related to early assistance and willing to engage in frank and open discussions about the topic.

We identified four mass adverse events to use as case studies of how some PRPs have responded in the wake of disasters that they may have played a role in creating. Popular media articles were used as sources of information for these incidents and as a means to obtain insight into stakeholder views, particularly those of victims.

Another component of our research involved conducting two "tabletop" exercises in which a detailed but hypothetical disaster scenario was described to a group of experts. The scenarios described the events leading up to a massive explosion at a fertilizer plant, the possible causes, and the short- and long-term impact on residents and businesses, both locally and regionally. With the help of a facilitator, the group then discussed the various options available to stakeholders impacted by the incident.

Findings

What Are Some Examples of How Early Assistance Has Played Out in Practice?

We chose four illustrative instances where early assistance was offered by a PRP in the aftermath of a serious adverse event:

- CSX Transportation (CSX) tank-car derailment involving acrylonitrile (Tennessee, 2015)
- Pacific Gas and Electric (PG&E) natural gas explosion (California, 2010)
- Arkema organic peroxide combustion (Texas, 2017)
- *Athos I* oil spill (New Jersey, 2004).

We chose events that affected communities in ways that would likely trigger nontrivial claims by affected individuals, businesses, and governmental bodies, such as events involving property damage, business disruption, evacuation-related losses, expenditures for cleanup or first responders, or personal injuries. Descriptions of each incident include details of the circumstances leading up to the adverse event as well as its litigation history.

Table S.1 summarizes the key aspects and consequences of the four incidents examined. In all four cases, PRPs provided early assistance as we have defined it for the purposes of this paper, although in the Arkema incident, assistance efforts became a source of dissatisfaction and a focus of community frustration. Also, the assistance provided in the *Athos I* oil spill was shaped by a particular statutory framework that applies to the release of petroleum products in navigable waters of the United States and thus is different in nature than the types of early assistance in the other three examples. Litigation was prevalent in the CSX, PG&E, and Arkema incidents (releases of liability were not required to receive early assistance in these three incidents), and class actions were filed in both the CSX and Arkema incidents. In contrast, there was surprisingly little litigation in the *Athos I* oil spill, given its profound impact on the surrounding region. It is difficult to determine the extent to which early assistance affected litigation and regulatory outcomes. It appears that early assistance contributed to the denial of

Table S.1
Key Features of Four Early Assistance Examples

Incident (State, Year)	Types of Impacts, Damages, and Injuries	Types of Early Assistance	Litigation by Injured Parties	Government Litigation and Sanctions	Possible Impact of Early Assistance on Litigation and Sanctions
CSX tank-car derailment involving acrylonitrile (Tennessee, 2015)	5,000 evacuated; 200 treated for injuries; 46 admitted to hospital; 1 death claimed	Lodging vouchers; food and water; evacuation expenses; remediation of soil contamination	5 putative class actions alleging various losses, including property damage, environmental damage, and personal injury; 10 cases for personal injury and wrongful death	None uncovered	Judge ruled early assistance reduced pool of individuals with potential claims, which contributed to the denial of class certification in one case
PG&E natural gas pipeline explosion (California, 2010)	8 killed; 58 injured; 38 homes destroyed; 70 homes damaged; 300 homes evacuated	Costs of losses not covered by insurance; $15K to $50K per household depending on extent of damage; home rebuilding or purchase program; reimbursement of local-government response costs	180 cases involving over 500 plaintiffs ultimately filed, including claims for wrongful death, personal injury, property damage, nuisance, and emotional distress; criminal charges filed in federal court	$1.6 billion fine assessed against PRP by California Public Utilities Commission	Administrative law judges acknowledged PG&E's early assistance program in setting penalty; however, there is no clear evidence that the early assistance efforts carried any weight in the calculation of award size

Table S.1—Continued

Incident (State, Year)	Types of Impacts, Damages, and Injuries	Types of Early Assistance	Litigation by Injured Parties	Government Litigation and Sanctions	Possible Impact of Early Assistance on Litigation and Sanctions
Arkema organic peroxide combustion (Texas, 2017)	205 residents evacuated	Hotel vouchers; rental cars; gift cards for food, clothing, and medicine; pet care; debris and ash removal	Civil suits by named residents and first responders for personal injuries, loss of earning capacity, mental anguish, real and personal property damaged, etc.; putative class action on behalf of residents and first responders	Civil action for violating various govt. codes; criminal case against Arkema management	None detected
Athos I oil spill (New Jersey, 2004)	Temporarily shut down port of Philadelphia; affected onshore facilities; killed an estimated 12,000 birds; and fouled vessels, structures, and equipment along shore	Over 650 public and private damage claims, including claims for loss in business; PRP paid out $180 million in total cleanup costs, claims, and ship damages	Putative class action for property damage, economic loss, inconvenience, and diminished real estate value; the case was dismissed	United States filed suit seeking reimbursement of payments from Oil Spill Liability Trust Find	Payments through the OPA process resulted in surprisingly few lawsuits.

NOTE: OPA = Oil Pollution Act of 1990.

the certification of a class action in the CSX claim by reducing the number of injured parties with outstanding uncompensated claims. It may well be that PG&E's aggressive early assistance program reduced fines levied by the California Public Utility Commission compared with what they would have been otherwise, but it is difficult to be sure. The early assistance program in the Arkema case appears to have had little impact on public and private litigation (as well as on criminal prosecution activity), but that may be partly because its early assistance program was not well received. Finally, in the case of the *Athos I* oil spill, the Oil Pollution Act of 1990 (OPA) framework appears to have been effective in limiting private litigation at least, but as evident from the *Deepwater Horizon* spill, such success is not guaranteed.

What Are the Perceived Benefits and Drawbacks of Early Assistance from the Viewpoints of Different Stakeholders?

Table S.2 summarizes stakeholder perceptions of the potential benefits and drawbacks of early assistance. Descriptions of the incidents and the reactions of stakeholders make it clear that the implementation of early assistance is not an unquestionably beneficial strategy for PRPs, at least not in terms of always reducing future litigation or improving public opinion. And we heard concerns that early assistance relies on the uncertain assumption that corporations will refrain from taking advantage of victims at a very vulnerable time in their lives. However, there was an overall sense among those interviewed that PRP-provided early assistance was the "right thing to do" and can have a positive impact on outcomes.

What Are Various Options for Encouraging PRPs to Provide Early Assistance?

If policymakers want to encourage PRPs to provide early assistance following events, there are a number of actions they might take, such as

- explicitly including early assistance as a consideration in sentencing guidelines for criminal conduct
- considering early assistance when determining civil statutory sanctions

Table S.2
Potential Benefits and Drawbacks of Early Assistance Identified by Stakeholder Groups

Stakeholder Group	Potential Benefits	Potential Drawbacks
Potentially Responsible Parties (PRPs)	• Is the right thing to do • Improves public relations • Reduces litigation for property damage and economic loss (but not for personal injury) • Offers, at least, the potential to reduce criminal and civil sanctions and the amount of punitive damages • By stabilizing community, allows the company to resume normal operations more quickly	• It can be perceived as implicit acceptance of legal responsibility • Insurers might balk at reimbursing outlays for early assistance • It would not affect high-value claims but could result in paying more parties with low-value losses • Class action litigation would proceed regardless, and settlement value could be insensitive to early assistance efforts • It could generate negative publicity if problems occurred in the disbursement process or if some victims turned away • It lacks a predictable link between early assistance and post-event sanctions
Insurers	• Does not play out well in the long run to deny responsibility • Removes low-value claims quickly and reduces PRP defense costs in the long run	• None identified
Victims	• Can fill gaps in available assistance • Can distribute aid with minimal paperwork • May not require liability release	• Not all victims will take necessary steps to obtain available assistance • It may not be enough to fix a company's compromised image

Table S.2—Continued

Stakeholder Group	Potential Benefits	Potential Drawbacks
Plaintiff Attorneys	• Is the right thing to do • Can reduce suffering and disruption caused by the event	• It can be used by the company in an attempt to reduce punitive damage awards or to spend its way out of trouble • Vulnerable recipients may believe that early assistance is all the relief they are eligible to receive • It can reduce the willingness of the plaintiff attorney to take cases and the total assistance ultimately received by victims

- clarifying how post-incident behavior affects punitive damages
- applying OPA-like frameworks to high-risk industries.

Below, we consider each in turn.

Explicitly Including Early Assistance in Sentencing Guidelines for Criminal Conduct

The Federal Sentencing Guidelines provide U.S. District Court judges with an assessment tool to help them decide sentences for corporations found guilty of criminal conduct. The guidelines reduce the severity of potential sentences when the corporation's actions before and after the incident evidence that an "effective compliance and ethics program" was in place.[1] Section 8B2.1(b)(7) of the guidelines indicates that judges should determine whether the organization took "reasonable steps" to respond appropriately to what happened. In 2010, the U.S. Sentencing Commission proposed that the following comment be added to the guidelines, to make it clear that a company seeking a

1 U.S. Sentencing Commission, 2018, § 8B2.1.

downward adjustment in any potential criminal sentence must have taken reasonable steps to address the harm caused to victims:

> First, the organization should respond appropriately to the criminal conduct. In the event the criminal conduct has an identifiable victim or victims the organization should take reasonable steps to provide restitution and otherwise remedy the harm resulting from the criminal conduct. Other appropriate responses may include self-reporting, cooperation with authorities, and other forms of remediation.[2] (emphasis added)

The public was then given an opportunity to comment on the proposed comment. While many were in favor of making the requirement more explicit, as the commission suggested, others argued that ". . . it would be unreasonable to expect restitution where, for example, civil litigation has not run its course and identifiable victims will not release claims as part of a proposed restitution payment."[3]

In the end, a watered-down version was adopted, in which there was no absolute duty to provide restitution when victims could be identified. In essence, it would be up to the company to determine whether restitution was "appropriate."[4] Adopting the guidance originally proposed by the commission would have been one way to incentivize early assistance, making it clear to a company that had found itself as a potential point of origin for a widespread disaster that an aggressive aid program might hedge against receiving the maximum possible criminal sentence.

---

[2] 75 Fed. Reg. 3534 (January 21, 2010).

[3] Gibson Dunn, 2010.

[4] "First, the organization should respond appropriately to the criminal conduct. The organization should take reasonable steps, as warranted under the circumstances, to remedy the harm resulting from the criminal conduct. These steps may include, where appropriate, providing restitution to identifiable victims, as well as other forms of remediation. Other reasonable steps to respond appropriately to the criminal conduct may include self-reporting and cooperation with authorities." U.S. Sentencing Comm'n, 2018, § 8B2.1, *Commentary*, effective November 1, 2010.

Considering Early Assistance When Determining Civil Statutory Sanctions

To promote early assistance, it might help to revise current civil penalty policies to account for PRP efforts to provide voluntary assistance to an affected community; for example, by engaging in aggressive cleanup operations and testing of soil, water, and air. One such revision might be to add a consideration to the penalty-calculating algorithms regarding the degree to which early assistance helped return a community to some semblance of normality. As a result, a good-faith effort that is appropriately sized could become the basis of a downward adjustment in any penalty, similar to what now can result when a regulated entity voluntarily agrees to undertake supplemental environmental projects.

Another way to encourage early assistance might be to include early assistance as a type of offset to the economic-benefit component of the penalty. Environmental Protection Agency (EPA) guidance for certain Clean Water Act (CWA) violations state that the economic-benefit component is intended to place "violators in the same financial position as they would have been if they had complied on time" with applicable regulations. The value of early assistance (such as the dollars spent by a PRP for contractors to visit affected homes and remove toxic substances on the properties) could be subtracted from the economic-benefit subtotal.

Finally, early assistance could be factored into the gravity component of the penalty-determination process. The EPA's assessment of the gravity of CWA violations is essentially intended both as a punitive measure and as a deterrent against similar bad behavior by ensuring that the regulated entity is actually worse off than it would have been had it simply obeyed the law in the first place. Current EPA guidance also provides for certain "gravity adjustment factors" that can enhance or reduce overall gravity calculations. One such factor is a "Quick Settlement Adjustment." EPA's civil penalty policy states that in "order to provide an extra incentive for violators to negotiate quickly and reasonably, and in recognition of a violator's cooperativeness," the agency can reduce the overall gravity by 10 percent if it "expects the violator to settle quickly." A similar gravity-adjustment factor that instead considers whether the violator initiated a good-faith early assistance program would presumably incentivize a party's interest in rapidly addressing the consequences of its actions.

Clarifying How Post-Incident Behavior Affects Punitive Damages

Early assistance might be encouraged if PRPs knew that quickly taking the appropriate action to help disaster victims could reduce their financial exposure, should litigation ensue and result in an award of punitive damages. However, the law concerning the extent to which post-incident behaviors by a PRP can affect the size of the punitive damage award is far from settled. The decades-long litigation over punitive damages in the *Exxon Valdez* case did not conclude with any clear guidance by the Supreme Court on the extent to which Exxon's payments to victims after the oil spill should enter into the calculation of the size of punitive damages. Guidance to the triers of fact when determining the size of a punitive damage verdict varies a great deal across states; however, some states provide models that might be used as a starting point for creating an express statutory requirement that considers the post-event behavior of defendants in the context of punitive damages.

Given that the legal authority for assessing punitive damages is, for the most part, the province of the legislatures and appellate courts of the individual states, moving toward a uniform, national standard, in which evidence of early assistance can be used to mitigate punitive damage awards, would probably not be easy. Nevertheless, a state interested in encouraging corporations within its borders to respond quickly and robustly to disasters potentially of their own making might consider reexamining its rules for assessing the size of punitive awards.

Applying OPA-Like Frameworks to High-Risk Industries

A fourth option for incentivizing early assistance involves applying a framework similar to that of the OPA to activities conducted in high-risk industries (other than those already within OPA jurisdiction, such as industries that transport, store, refine, extract, or use petroleum products). OPA appears to offer an efficient approach in dealing with thousands of discharges each year, the vast majority of which are handled in relative quiet, address consequences as a matter of routine, and keep victims from incurring high transaction costs to recover a wide range of damages. Perhaps a similar program could be set up for specific commercial activities for which a rapid response by PRPs is desired.

Concluding Thoughts

After weighing the benefits and drawbacks, policymakers may choose to encourage PRPs to play a role in providing early assistance. Tweaking the guidelines for corporate criminal sentencing, adjusting the severity of civil sanctions downward when the company conducts a good-faith early assistance program, and considering a company's mitigation efforts when deciding on the size of a punitive damage award are all ways that might encourage companies to provide early assistance. However, decisions on whether to push for such policies should also consider the extent to which any change in the law might provide well-financed companies with the luxury of spending their way out of a large fine or punitive damage award, which would undercut any deterrence against future bad behavior. Such decisions should also consider the potential for uncoordinated responses by multiple parties (i.e., PRPs, government, and nonprofits), which could result in duplication of effort and waste.

Policymakers may be legitimately concerned that increasing incentives for early assistance could result in unwanted consequences, but there may be ways to mitigate those concerns. One way might be to give the greatest weight to early assistance provided the very first day of the incident—when the need is most acute and liability most uncertain—and the least weight to aid rolled out after many months, once investigative reports are in and lawyers are deep into the pretrial process. Efforts of smaller enterprises could be assessed not by how much money they spend but by the degree to which they cooperate with governmental agencies and participate in recovery efforts over the long haul. No doubt there are other strategies, but, ultimately, the entire spectrum of stakeholders (PRPs, the plaintiffs' bar, liability insurers, regulators, etc.) must collaborate to determine the best ways to retain the traditional deterrence mechanisms of sanctions, fines, and punitive awards, while promoting the idea of early assistance and accelerating the pace at which a community gets back on its feet.

Acknowledgments

We wish to thank those who participated in our expert interviews for their patience in answering our seemingly endless questions and their graciousness in providing answers that were both frank and helpful. We also appreciate the intellectual contributions of members of the RAND Center for Catastrophic Risk Management and Compensation's Advisory Board and the RAND Institute for Civil Justice's Board of Overseers during their participation in disaster simulations, which helped us to think about key issues.

Lynn Everett did an excellent job of editing and organizing the final version of this document. We would also like to thank our formal reviewers, Samuel L. Tarry, Jr. and Geoffrey R. McGovern, for their extremely thoughtful reviews and constructive comments. The authors retain full responsibility for any remaining errors.

Abbreviations

ALJ	administrative law judge
CPUC	California Public Utility Commission
CSX	CSX Transportation
CWA	Clean Water Act
EPA	Environmental Protection Agency
FEMA	Federal Emergency Management Agency
FRA	Federal Railway Administration
FRE	Federal Rule of Evidence
NPFC	National Pollution Funds Center
OPA	Oil Pollution Act of 1990
OSLTF	Oil Spill Liability Trust Fund
PG&E	Pacific Gas and Electric Company
PRP	potentially responsible party
RP	responsible party
SADT	self-accelerating decomposition temperature
TCEQ	Texas Commission on Environmental Quality

CHAPTER ONE

Introduction

Responding to a Disaster

While the onset of a major disaster may be unpredictable, the response often involves a common sequence of actors and timing.[1] The most immediate assistance comes in the form of self-help, in which victims render first aid to themselves and those in their immediate surroundings and take steps to prevent further injury and property loss, such as extinguishing small fires, turning off gas lines, or sheltering in place. Neighbors and work colleagues are often the next to assist, perhaps by helping to cut up downed tree limbs on adjoining properties or offering a place to spend the night. First responders will eventually arrive to address critical public-safety needs, including rescue, recovery, medical assistance, fire suppression, and law enforcement. The National Guard may be called in to assist with those tasks as well. Nongovernmental organizations experienced in disaster relief, such as the Red Cross and the Salvation Army, are often next on the scene, providing shelter, food, and counseling. First-party insurers may set up mobile centers to dispense funds to policyholders covered for property damage, displacement expenses, or business interruption. Businesses and charitable organizations, located both locally and outside affected areas, may donate and deliver goods that are in short supply, such as dia-

[1] In this paper, we define *disaster* as a mass adverse event that unfolds rapidly and causes significant loss (such as property damage, financial loss, personal injury, or environmental damage) to many people or over a wide area, although we are mindful that *rapidly*, *significant*, *many*, and *wide* are certainly subjective terms.

pers, drinking water, and medical supplies. And in instances where the actual or threatened incident satisfied requirements of the Stafford Act and, in turn, triggered a presidential declaration of a major disaster or emergency, resources from the federal government come into play.[2] At this stage, the focus is on paving the way to long-term recovery, often through assistance grants, low-interest disaster loans, funds to make homes safe and habitable, and reimbursements to local and state agencies for expenses related to emergency protective measures and debris removal. Other governmental programs, such as state workers' compensation systems, the Social Security Administration, Medicaid, and Medicare, may also play a role.

When a disaster is suspected to have an anthropogenic origin (i.e., the disaster was caused or its effects were exacerbated by the actions or inactions of persons or entities), the U.S. system of tort liability can also play a role in the recovery process. Those impacted adversely by the event may eventually seek to recover their losses from the alleged tortfeasors, advancing demands for compensation or other relief, either directly—with those believed to be responsible—or with the third-party liability insurers for those parties. Though such claims can be made without the assistance of legal counsel, the complexity of issues involving proof of liability and the calculation of damages often provides sufficient incentive to seek the advice of an attorney. In some instances, claims may evolve into disputes that lead to formal litigation and perhaps even trial.

The Role of the Tort System

There are three aspects of the tort liability process that most notably differentiate it from other post-disaster responses. One aspect involves the wide variety of monetary damages that can be sought from an alleged tortfeasor. Assistance from neighbors, fire departments, charitable organ-

[2] The Disaster Relief and Emergency Assistance Amendments of 1988, Pub. L. No. 100-707, 102 Stat 4689 (1988). The Energy Policy Act of 2005, Pub. L. No. 109-58, 119 Stat 594 (2005).

izations, governmental agencies, and others responding to the emergency are obviously vital, but they are also limited in scope and generally focused on stabilizing the unfolding situation so that no further harm is incurred, ending immediate threats, and temporarily providing for basic human needs. As a result, the long-term responsibilities for rebuilding damaged homes, reopening shuttered businesses, dealing with the ongoing impact of disaster-related medical conditions, replacing or repairing personal property, surviving interruptions in work income, cleaning up debris, and the like are primarily those of a disaster's victims. While first-party insurance can help in this regard, and while government agencies may offer some financial assistance, the former source requires the victim to have had the foresight and financial capability to obtain such coverage before the onset of the disaster, and the latter sources typically provide their most generous monetary help for rebuilding in the form of low-interest loans that eventually must be paid back.[3]

In contrast, claimants who have been successful in asserting that others bear at least some liability for the consequences of a disaster have the potential to receive compensation addressing, for example, past and future medical expenses, reductions in past and future earnings, the costs of repairing or replacing damaged real and personal property, reductions in income related to the use of property (such as rent payments), losses related to potential employment or business opportunities, and the loss of financial support from family members who were killed as a result of the disaster. Moreover, the U.S. system of jurisprudence also allows claimants to seek what are often referred to as noneconomic or general damages—losses that cannot be easily measured by the value of an invoice or a bank statement but are no less real, such as pain, suffering, emotional distress, loss of companionship, and other consequences that can accompany personal injuries or death. In other words, compensation available through tort law is designed to make a victim of a disaster "whole as nearly as that may be done by an award

---

[3] In particularly large disasters, Congress can authorize large amounts of assistance through the Community Block Grant Program administered by the U.S. Department of Housing and Urban Development. These grant programs are typically focused on lower-income households.

of money."[4] In terms of fully restoring the *status quo ante*, tort liability may be the most powerful post-disaster response available, as long as there are liable parties with adequate resources to cover the damages.

But a second key distinction between tort and other forms of post-disaster response is that, in the former, the process to obtain compensation is adversarial in nature. Corporations, government agencies, and individuals who are perceived to be potentially responsible parties (PRPs), or legally liable for harms rendered by the disaster, may have a very different view of their roles in triggering the event or causing related losses.[5] Even when PRPs are aware that their ability to avoid civil or criminal liability over the long run is highly doubtful, they may adopt strategies to minimize their financial exposure in every way practical. Their attorneys, characterized by some as highly risk-averse as a result of being "trained from the first day of law school to give advice that 'protects' their clients," may recommend taking no action, as action might imply an acknowledgment of responsibility or result in an inadvertent disclosure that could be offered later as proof of negligence or other questionable behavior.[6] Such strategies can include running silent in the event's aftermath, declining to comment on questions posed by the media, referring the inquiries of regulators or law enforcement to legal counsel, and essentially ignoring all requests for compensation until being forced to respond as a result of formal litigation. An alternative approach involves mounting a highly aggressive public defense almost from the moment the dust has settled, loudly pointing the finger at others, including suppliers, vendors, subcontractors, business partners, government regulators, Mother Nature, and occasionally the victims themselves. In such instances, compensation claims may go unresolved until the PRP is required to pay up as a result of a negotiated settlement or the judgment of the court. In contrast,

---

4 *Yoshioka v. Superior Court*, 58 Cal. App. 4th 972, 997 (Cal. Ct. App., 1997).

5 In this paper, we use the term *potentially responsible party* in a generic sense. That term can have a very specific legal meaning, particularly with regard to Environmental Protection Agency (EPA) enforcement activities, but here we simply mean an actor that may bear some adjudicated responsibility for the cause or severity of a mass adverse event.

6 Rizer, 2015, p. 952.

much of the post-disaster aid rendered by charitable organizations, first responders, and others is freely given, and it is obtained with little or no action on victims' part.

A final distinction between tort and other forms of compensation concerns the related concepts of time and uncertainty. After the initial impact of an event, even though it might take first responders only minutes to arrive, thereafter, it can take an extremely long time before a person or organization accused of contributing to the onset of a disaster is determined legally liable with finality and any compensation actually paid. Though the first claims against PRPs may be advanced almost immediately (it is not unknown for attorneys and their clients to publicly announce the filing of a lawsuit within a day or two of the adverse event), if the claim is not dropped or settled, the matter can proceed to trial, an event that, depending on the location of court and the complexity of the issues (which are a hallmark of disaster-related litigation), might not take place for many years.

That lengthy process also raises the specter of uncertainty, in which a victim's eligibility for compensation and the amount, if any, are by no means predictable. Though there are often complaints related to submitting applications to agencies, insurers, and charities when seeking loans, benefits, grants, or other financial assistance (e.g., onerous paperwork requirements and confusing policies), at least disaster victims have some general sense of whether such aid is available, whether they are qualified candidates, and how much money they may be entitled to receive. Tort claimants have no such assurances, and what might appear at first glance to be a fairly open-and-shut case regarding liability can morph into a pitched battle—over complex scientific and technical questions, over the legal connection between the actions of others and the victim's losses, and between multiple alleged tortfeasors who are all seeking to put the blame on each other. Moreover, the uncertainly of success and the hefty transaction costs that can be incurred in that pursuit (e.g., attorney's fees, expert witness fees, and other expenses) can serve to influence disaster victims to drop claims or even decline to seek compensation in the first place.

Nevertheless, it is not unknown for PRPs to address at least some of the effects of a disaster in the relatively early days following the onset of the event, even though their doing so might be seen by some as an implicit admission of guilt, and even though the very real question of who is responsible remains to be determined. Examples of this type of early assistance to disaster victims can be found in railroad derailment incidents, where some of the contents of freight cars or tank cars escape, potentially placing those in proximity in harm's way. It is not unusual for a railway to offer hotel and restaurant vouchers to those living in the affected area immediately after government authorities have issued evacuation orders. It is also not unusual for the railway to make such an offer freely, without requiring victims to waive any future rights to seek compensation for other derailment-related losses that might occur. One might argue that these sorts of accidents are very special incidents from a liability standpoint, because the responsibility for the leakage of fumes or other substances appears to be unquestionably upon the shoulders of the railway. In actuality, there can be legitimate questions of law and fact in regard to a railway's liability in such cases, particularly if the derailment was a result of arguably unforeseen acts, such as when motor vehicles enter the right-of-way and cause a collision, when vandals strike (breaking into locked railway facilities and throwing electronically controlled track switches, for example), or when an internal defect in the track was undetected despite the use of proper, industry-standard inspection techniques such as ultrasound scans. In the initial days following the derailment, a railway may decide that it makes sense to help those affected as soon as possible, even though the underlying cause is still a matter of speculation and a more thorough analysis later might suggest, from a legal standpoint, that the derailment was not its fault. Indeed, in many such derailment instances, railways have quickly offered their help to address at least some of the immediate needs of local residents and businesses but then, for years afterward, as additional aspects of liability wound their way through the courts, aggressively defended the company's interests.

Examining Early Assistance

This paper examines instances in which businesses with a potential connection to the cause or magnitude of an adverse event have taken steps to address some of the initial consequences of the event and its impact on individuals, organizations, and communities—even when the precise nature of legal responsibility remains unsettled. That assistance could include, for example,

- handing out hotel vouchers to those subject to evacuation orders
- sending out teams to replace shattered windows
- providing cash payments to offset the inconvenience of utility disruptions or to buy clothing
- distributing food and water
- arranging for rental cars
- paying for the removal of hazardous materials from private properties
- reimbursing emergency room bills
- arranging pet care
- covering local and state government costs of first responders
- donating to charitable organizations that are already providing relief to victims of the disaster
- bringing in mobile pharmacies
- conducting water-supply and soil testing on demand
- covering business-interruption losses
- assisting in transportation needs
- paying for home repairs
- setting up large-scale claims facilities.

We describe such aid as a form of "assistance" rather than "compensation" because the signature feature of compensation as a form of *quid pro quo,* in which money is given in exchange for releasing a party from potential tort liability, may not always be present. An offer of assistance might, for example, have no purpose other than to ameliorate the suffering of others. We also characterize this assistance as being "early" in its timing, as it is provided (or at least offered) relatively soon after the onset of the event and long before the business obligated to make such provision as the result of the settlement of tort claims or the judgment of a court of law.

Our interest in early assistance arises from its potential to speed recovery, reduce the overall losses caused by an event, and reduce litigation and related transaction costs. To this end, this study addresses three main questions:

1. What are some examples of how early assistance has played out in practice?
2. What are the perceived advantages and downsides of early assistance from the viewpoints of different stakeholders, including victims, PRPs, insurers, and counsel?
3. If early assistance is deemed useful, what are various options for encouraging PRPs to provide early assistance?

Our goals here are limited. This paper is not intended to serve as a comprehensive analysis of any fundamental issue in disaster response, relief, and recovery. Rather, we simply hope to stimulate a conversation about the optimal role a PRP may have in providing aid to a community that appears to have been adversely affected by its actions.

Approach

We initially reviewed controlling legal authority with a focus on the evidentiary implications of PRP actions in any assessment of liability following an adverse event. Secondary legal literature (law review articles, legal treatises, etc.), legal periodicals, and topical guides were searched as well.

We also conducted a series of semistructured, not-for-attribution interviews with outside counsel for corporations who had been PRPs in the past, in-house counsel for similar entities, plaintiffs' attorneys, special masters, academics, and insurers. The interviewees were purposely selected to reflect a broad range of stakeholder and expert groups, and we targeted candidates who were knowledgeable about issues related to early assistance and willing to engage in frank and open discussions about the topic.

We identified four mass adverse events to use as case studies of how some PRPs have responded in the wake of disasters that they may have played a role in creating. Popular media articles, governmental reports, and legal documents were used as sources of information for these incidents and as a means to obtain insight into stakeholder views, particularly those of victims.

Another component of our research involved conducting two "tabletop" exercises in which a detailed but hypothetical disaster scenario was described to a group of experts.[7] The scenarios described the events leading up to a massive explosion at a fertilizer plant, the possible causes, and the short-and long-term impact on residents and businesses, both locally and regionally. With the help of a facilitator, the group then discussed the various options available to stakeholders impacted by the incident. The ramifications of possible actions that might be taken by PRPs at the center of the incident were debated by the expert group, and the facilitator varied the "facts" of the underlying hypotheticals to see how the comments and positions of the participants might change.

Organization of This Paper

Chapter Two, in order to inform the discussions in subsequent chapters, describes four real-world examples of early assistance along with observations on the outcomes of each. Chapter Three sets forth what we learned about the perspectives of various stakeholder groups (such as disaster victims, PRPs, insurers, and plaintiffs' attorneys) regarding the potential benefits and downsides to the provision of early assistance. Chapter Four describes some possible options for encouraging PRPs to provide assistance in the initial days following a disaster. And Chapter Five provides concluding thoughts.

---

[7] The experts used in the initial exercise were attendees at an Advisory Board meeting of the RAND Center for Catastrophic Risk Management and Compensation. The board is made up a diverse group of legal, academic, and organizational experts in preventing and addressing the consequences of disasters, including judges, professors, members of the mass tort plaintiffs' bar, insurance professionals, and members of the corporate counsel and outside defense counsel bar. The second exercise was held at a meeting of the Board of Overseers for the RAND Institute for Civil Justice. The institute's board includes plaintiffs' lawyers, defense lawyers, judicial officers, insurers, and representatives from other industries and from consumer and labor groups.

CHAPTER TWO

How Early Assistance Works in Practice

The four illustrative examples that follow describe instances where early assistance was offered by a PRP in the aftermath of a serious adverse event. The examples include

- a train derailment and subsequent toxic smoke release
- a natural gas explosion in a residential neighborhood
- a manufacturing plant emergency involving unstable chemicals
- an oil spill in an inland waterway.

We chose events that affected communities in ways that would be likely to trigger nontrivial claims by affected individuals, businesses, and governmental bodies, such as those involving property damage, business disruption, evacuation-related losses, expenditures for cleanup or first responders, or personal injuries. The descriptions that follow include detailed background on the circumstances leading up to the adverse event as well as its litigation history.

It should be noted that the four examples are not intended to represent the universe of disasters. They were purposively selected as examples of instances where the incident had taken place within the past 15 years, the underlying event could be considered a human-caused disaster from the perspective of the affected community, and there were media reports of early assistance offered by a PRP. We chose to employ a case study approach because it can provide a better understanding of a complex social phenomenon (PRP-provided early assistance) as a result of selecting examples of that phenomenon, subjecting those examples to close scrutiny, and identifying points of similarity and divergence.

Example 1: CSX Transportation Tank-Car Derailment

The Incident and Aftermath

Just before midnight on July 1, 2015, a CSX Transportation (CSX) freight train derailed near the city limits of Maryville, Tennessee, a community of nearly 30,000 residents located in the eastern part of the state in Blount County, about 16 miles south of Knoxville.[1] To be precise, it was a single tank car in the 57-car train that derailed, but that particular piece of equipment (manufactured and owned by the Union Tank Car Company) happened to be carrying about 24,000 gallons of liquid acrylonitrile. The chemical has a wide variety of uses—it is a key component of the plastics used to make residential sewage pipes and Lego toys, for example—but it is particularly dangerous. It is highly flammable, potentially carcinogenic, and toxic at even low dosages, and when ignited, its fumes contain both hydrogen cyanide and nitrogen oxides. Unfortunately, the cargo indeed ignited, triggering a fire that continued to burn for about 19 hours and sending a thick plume of noxious smoke over parts of western Blount County.

City and county police and fire departments were first on the scene, followed by resources from the Tennessee Emergency Management Agency. The incident triggered an evacuation of about 5,000 people, who lived or worked within two miles of the crash site. Police officers knocked on the doors of area residents and businesses throughout the morning of July 2, urging them to leave immediately. Almost 200 people (including about ten first responders) were eventually treated at local medical facilities, with 46 admitted to a hospital.

---

[1] The description of the events surrounding this incident was derived from the following sources: Beecken, 2016; CSX, 2015a; CSX, 2015b; CSX, 2015c; *Daily Times*, 2017; Megargee and Clark, 2015; Mondlock, 2015; Slaby, 2015; and U.S. Department of Transportation, 2017.

By 5:00 a.m. on July 2, the Red Cross had set up a shelter on the campus of a local school and began registering evacuees. Shortly thereafter, CSX established what it characterized as a "community outreach center" at the same site, and with the help of CSX personnel and volunteers, the company began to hand out lodging vouchers to displaced residents. CSX also provided food, bottled water, refreshments, pet care, and access to prescription medications as well as forms for submitting requests to the railroad for evacuation-expense reimbursements. According to local newspaper reports, some "evacuated residents were pleasantly surprised by hotel vouchers and an abundance of food and free ice cream."[2] The railroad also set up a call center (described as a "community resource hotline") to provide information to those affected by the event.

An emergency response company hired by CSX arrived during the morning to address the environmental consequences of the event, and later that day tankers and heavy equipment were brought in to help with the cleanup and remove the train. Tests performed on behalf of CSX sampled ground water at various locations as well as the interiors and exteriors of local school busses, but the presence of toxic chemicals initially came up negative.

By the morning of July 3, the worst of the immediate effects were over. The evacuation orders were lifted that day (though many residents did not return until at least July 4), and by noon only the burned tank car and a second tanker, which also contained acrylonitrile, remained at the incident site. These two cars were removed by the next day. CSX's outreach center continued to operate until evening, and after that point assistance for reimbursements and the like were provided through the call center and downloadable claim forms.

By the end of August, CSX had removed all of the contaminated soil from the derailment site, but follow-up testing of some wells in the area showed low levels of acrylonitrile. CSX ran temporary waterlines to those served by the affected wells, offered reimbursements for the costs of obtaining alternative water sources, and brought in equipment

---

2 Megargee and Clark, 2015.

to drill deep enough to test the ground water. The executive director of the Tennessee Clean Water Network indicated that she was pleased to see CSX providing water and expense reimbursements but hoped the company would take responsibility for the continued impact of the problems, arguing that testing should continue for at least a year. CSX treated the affected wells at various points during the next two years with injections of persulfate and sodium hydroxide; and as a result, state officials reported significant reductions in the levels of acrylonitrile.

Within a few months of the derailment, Blount County, Maryville, and the nearby city of Alcoa sought to recover expenditures for first responders, administrative services, utilities, command center expenses, and other supplies. Maryville's city manager noted that "CSX has been very cooperative in providing the resources needed to effectively manage the train derailment," and that there was every reason to believe the city would be made whole for its expenditures.[3] The finance director for Alcoa voiced similar expectations. By July of 2016, it was reported that "CSX had paid out more than $3.5 million to local governments, community organizations, medical providers and individuals to reimburse expenses incurred as a result of the derailment" and had "removed more than 4,900 tons of soil, liquid and other contaminated materials at a cost of $3.1 million."[4]

In November 2017, the Federal Railway Administration (FRA) issued its accident-investigation report concerning the incident. The FRA concluded that the probable cause of the derailment was the sudden overheating and subsequent failure of a roller bearing on an axle of the tank car. The derailment itself then led to the axle breaking and a wheel coming in contact with the shell of the tank car and breaching the exterior. Leakage of the contents, combined with sparks or excessive heat buildup from steel-on-steel friction, was believed to have ignited the acrylonitrile. What led to the roller bearing overheating was not identified in the FRA report, but the investigators did rule out track conditions, the qualifications and conditions of the train crew, and the

---

3 Bales-Sherrod, 2015.

4 *Daily Times*, 2017.

manner in which the train was operated. Maintenance records revealed no indication of any prior problem with the roller bearings or axles on the tank car. Notably, the train had passed by a properly operating "hot box" detector about 45 minutes prior to the derailment. (Hot boxes are sensors located adjacent to the track at regular points along rail lines for the purpose of identifying axle-bearing overheating and other defects and, if required, alerting the crew to any problem.) No issues were reported or recorded by the detector, and, as such, the FRA characterized the overheating as "sudden."

Legal Developments

The first lawsuits began a little more than a week after the derailment.[5] A putative class action was filed in Blount County Circuit Court on July 10, seeking class treatment for potentially more than 5,000 residents in and around Maryville who were subject to evacuation orders or had a possessory interest in property within the evacuation zone. CSX was the sole defendant in this action, and damages sought were limited to losses arising from the evacuation itself (such as the loss of use or enjoyment of real property, inconvenience, out-of-pocket expenses, the loss of income, and related mental and emotional injuries); they did not cover physical injuries or property damage related to the toxic fumes. Attorneys for the named plaintiffs in the action acknowledged their appreciation for the outreach efforts of CSX but indicated that they, nevertheless, "filed this lawsuit because we really want to make sure that those affected by this accident are fully and fairly compensated for the disruption this has caused to their lives."[6]

Another putative class action was filed the following month, though in this instance the venue was in federal district court and the losses that were alleged included those resulting from property damage, environmental damage, and personal injuries as a result of

---

[5] The description of the legal history surrounding this incident was derived from the following sources: Beecken, 2016; Crowe, 2015; Wade, 2016; Wade, 2017; Wade, 2018; and complaints and other pleadings and papers filed in related lawsuits.

[6] Crowe, 2015.

the toxic fumes and related evacuation. The federal case expanded the defendant pool to include CSX and Union Tank Car.

A week later, four sheriff's deputies and six police officers also filed suit in federal district court (each as individual plaintiffs). They sought compensation for personal injuries related to their extended exposure to the fumes as a result of being dispatched to the affected area to assist in the evacuations. As with the putative class action, the suit involving law-enforcement personnel listed both CSX and Union Tank Car as defendants.

Over the next few years, additional lawsuits commenced in state and federal courts, some on behalf of individually named plaintiffs and others seeking class certification in order to advance claims on behalf of unidentified individuals. Five such suits were filed in Blount County Circuit Court just before the first anniversary of the derailment, presumably related to the fact that Tennessee has a one-year statute of limitations for personal injury actions.[7] One was an action seeking $20 million in damages for the wrongful death of a local fire department captain who passed away in October 2015, alleging that CSX had failed to notify first responders of the contents of the derailed tank car until two hours had passed, during which time the captain had been exposed to the fumes and sustained severe injuries. In addition to CSX and Union Tank Car, the train's engineer and conductor were named as defendants. The same four defendants were named in another of the first-year anniversary filings, this one a putative class action seeking $80 million for personal injuries, property damages, and punitive damages on behalf of area residents.

Of the approximately 15 cases ultimately brought against CSX and other defendants, five sought to represent a class of plaintiffs. Two of these putative class actions eventually settled on an individual basis, as the resolution affected only the handful of plaintiffs identified in the original complaint. The other three class actions were consolidated into a single lawsuit seeking remediation for property damages; aggravation and inconvenience; and fear, anxiety, and mental anguish. Remedia-

[7] Tenn. Code Ann. § 28-3-104(a)(1).

tion was sought for essentially all individuals within the evacuation zone on the night of the derailment, estimated by filing attorneys to be at least 5,000 in number, based on the area's population according to census data. When the motion for certifying a plaintiff class was eventually considered, the federal judge overseeing the consolidated matters decided against the plaintiffs. One of the necessary criteria for class treatment in a federal civil lawsuit is that the case must be one in which the number of potential class members would be so large as to make it impractical to name each individually in a single complaint (a rule commonly referred to as the *numerosity requirement*). The judge concluded that the estimates of potential class size offered by the plaintiffs' attorneys were essentially speculative and would be insufficient to satisfy the numerosity requirement. One reason given was that the estimates were based on the number of residents in the affected area, when, in fact, it would only be the number of people who were actually present and had uncompensated losses from the event. In the judge's view, the early assistance efforts of CSX had reduced the pool of individuals with legitimate claims to some unknown degree, adding to the uncertainty over the size of the proposed class:

> Furthermore, the Court notes that after the derailment, CSX established a community outreach and claims processing center to reimburse individuals for incurred expenses. Pursuant to this claims program, CSX made payments of $500 to over 1,000 households within the evacuation area. In addition to these payments, CSX submits that it made hundreds of thousands of dollars of additional payments to individuals within the evacuation zone by reimbursing them for out-of-pocket expenses and lodging at nearby hotels. CSX submits that it also provided food and water for evacuees, reimbursed local employees for lost wages, paid for claimed medical expenses, and made donations to local community organizations. While plaintiffs argue that these payments do not fully compensate purported class members for all incurred damages, and also that these numbers are lower than CSX has paid in previous class action settlements, it is likely that CSX's community outreach and claims program will affect the number of individuals within the evacuation zone with outstand-

> ing uncompensated claims. Indeed, another district court in an action with similar factual circumstances to the current case found that the defendants' establishment of a claim center suggested to the court that some residents who might otherwise fall within the class definition would not be class members because they had been fully compensated. See *In re Paulsboro Derailment Cases*, 2014 WL 4162790, at *8 (D.N.J. Aug. 20, 2014) ("[E]vidence exists suggesting that some remaining residents would not be class members. Defendants established an assistance center . . . where evacuees could obtain reimbursement for expenses as well as gift cards for future expenses, without signing releases.").[8] (citations and footnotes omitted)

Once the motion for class certification was denied, counsel for plaintiffs on the consolidated case had few options other than to continue the litigation on behalf of only the six named plaintiffs. A trial date was set, but shortly before it began, the six plaintiffs settled with CSX, leaving Union Tank Car as the remaining defendant at trial. In March 2018 a jury reached a verdict for the plaintiffs but awarded only a modest $13,213 in total damages (an average of about $2,200 per plaintiff). The award was based on a finding that the derailment had created a nuisance on each of the plaintiffs' real properties and that Union Tank Car was 40 percent at fault while CSX was responsible for the remaining 60 percent. (Despite CSX not being a formal defendant at the trial, the jury could still decide on the relative liabilities of all PRPs, though only Union Tank Car would be required to pay a share.) Interestingly, the jury found for the defendant (and by reference, for CSX as well) on the issue of negligence. The key result of this trial and the preceding denial of class certification is that, within four months of receiving the jury's verdict (and just prior to the end of the Tennessee three-year limitations on the filing of nuisance and property damage claims), the attorneys who had sought class treatment revised their strategy and filed a new lawsuit that named 384 separate plaintiffs. As

---

[8] Memorandum Opinion and Order, filed September 26, 2017, in *Tipton et al. v. CSX Transportation, Inc. et al.*, No. 3:15-cv-00311 (U.S. District Court, E.D. Tenn.).

this paper is written, that case is still active, as is the Blount County Circuit Court claim regarding the wrongful death of the fire captain.

Discussion

Railroads have considerable experience with handling the initial consequences of derailments. In 2017, for example, there were 1,253 derailments deemed significant enough to be reportable to the FRA, causing a total of $223 million in damages while killing three people and injuring 151.[9] They also have strong incentives to address those consequences rapidly and in a manner that is sensitive to the needs and perceptions of an affected community—because, while a railroad's rolling stock is constantly on the move, its track is immobile. Thus, it presumably makes good business sense to minimize the chance that residents and businesses will call for a rerouting of existing rail lines in the aftermath of an adverse incident.

Despite the absence of media reports describing any public dissatisfaction with the assistance that CSX provided to many of those living and working in Blount County, lawsuits seemed to begin as soon as the smoke cleared, and new ones were filed periodically. But those alleging personal injuries (and, in one instance, a death) involved consequences that were not likely to be the subject of CSX's activities in dispensing aid in the immediate days after the tank car caught on fire. The other suits—those focused on property damage, nuisance, aspects of the evacuation, or interruption in the normal course of business or personal life—would arguably involve claims that overlap with the types of losses that CSX attempted to offset by voluntarily providing "payments of $500 to over 1,000 households within the evacuation area"; reimbursing "hundreds of thousands of dollars" of "out-of-pocket expenses and lodging at nearby hotels" as well as "lost wages"; supplying "food and water for evacuees"; and paying for "claimed medical expenses." The record does not show the extent of such assistance on an individual basis, and it is conceivably possible that much of the CSX aid was inadequate compared with the actual non-personal-injury-related

---

9 Authors' analysis of FRA Office of Safety Analysis data available on the FRA website. See Federal Railroad Administration, undated.

losses incurred by those in the region; however, the very modest results of post-incident litigation, as evidenced by the individual plaintiff's trial verdicts, suggest that CSX might have already covered much of the "low-hanging fruit" in terms of local needs. Certainly the judge who denied class-action status appeared to suggest that many who accepted early assistance from CSX would fall out of the proposed class definition because their losses had already been covered to some extent—even though our research did not turn up evidence that CSX had required any sort of formal release in exchange for the provision of cash, vouchers, and the like.

Example 2: Pacific Gas and Electric Company Natural Gas Fire

The Incident and Aftermath

During the afternoon of Thursday, September 9, 2010, employees and contractors for Pacific Gas and Electric Company (PG&E), an energy utility serving northern California, were performing electrical work at the Milpitas Terminal, a PG&E local control station for the company's natural gas supply system in the San Francisco Bay Area.[10] A sequence of errors during the work led to the temporary loss of pressure control in the pipeline distribution system, resulting in higher-than-normal levels at points downstream from the terminal, including those in pipe segments running underneath San Bruno, a city about 12 miles south of San Francisco. While the increased pressure was far less than the rated maximums for the pipelines in the San Bruno area, it was enough to rupture a section identified as Segment 181. Later analysis revealed that Segment 181 was built in 1956 from a series of conjoined pipes and

[10] The description of events surrounding this incident was derived from the following sources: Bowe and Pickoff-White, 2015; CBS SF BayArea, 2010; Davidson et al., 2012; Jacobs Consultancy, 2011; Kindelan, 2010; Melvin, 2011; National Transportation Safety Board, 2011; Pacific Gas and Electric, 2010a; Pacific Gas and Electric, 2010b; Pacific Gas and Electric, 2010c; Pacific Gas and Electric, 2010d; Pacific Gas and Electric, 2012; San Mateo County Office of Emergency Services, 2012; Silverfarb, 2010; Soglin, 2010; Terrazas, 2011; and Van Derbeken, 2011, 2012.

that one of those components had a longitudinal seam that was only partially welded—a defect that should have been noted at the time of the original installation. That defect was believed to have weakened over time, and at 6:11 p.m. that day, the weld in Section 181 failed when subjected to the moderate increase in pressure.

The 28-ft-long, 3,000-lb. pipe section that ruptured was tossed 100 ft south of its original location, producing a crater measuring 72 ft by 26 ft. The escaping natural gas then ignited, triggering a giant fireball and flames that spread throughout the neighborhood. Because it took until about 7:30 p.m. before PG&E personnel confirmed that the explosion was the result of a gas-line problem and were able to close the valves in the vicinity of the breach, an estimated 47.6 million standard cubic feet of natural gas poured out of Section 181. The release of natural gas fed the fires, preventing first responders from approaching the source of the flames. By about 4:30 the next morning, the fires in the neighborhood were declared 75 percent contained, though hot spots remained until late the next day. Ultimately the explosion and fire killed eight people and injured 58 (ten of whom had injuries described as serious). It also led to the evacuation of residents in about 300 homes, destroying 38 of those homes and damaging 70 more (some of which were later determined to be uninhabitable).

Within a few hours after the explosion, an "evacuation center" was established to identify displaced residents and assess their immediate needs. Red Cross shelters were subsequently set up at two locations in San Bruno, offering food, water, a place to sleep, and, if needed, basic medical services. PG&E personnel helped to staff the aid sites and assisted with arrangements for temporary housing. Only about 39 victims actually spent that first night at any of the shelters (and none used the shelters on subsequent nights), with the low usage variously attributed to "the proximity of friends and family, the limited extent of the event, or the use of lodging vouchers paid by Pacific Gas and Electric."[11] Subsequently the shelters were consolidated into a single "local assistance center" (later developing into a "recovery center"),

[11] Davidson et al., 2012, p. 30.

where affected individuals could receive aid from PG&E, the Red Cross, and various nongovernmental organizations.

By Saturday, PG&E began to hand out gift cards worth $1,000 and vouchers for rental cars, which was in addition to the hotel vouchers it had already provided to those displaced by the explosion and fire. A vice president for the company indicated that PG&E was also prepared to compensate the families of those injured or killed and to provide long-term housing assistance, promising to "do everything we can to make you whole."[12]

On the following Monday, September 13, PG&E announced that it would set aside $100 million for the "Rebuild San Bruno Fund" as a means of providing "both immediate and long-term support to San Bruno residents and the city."[13] PG&E's press release described three primary purposes for the new fund:

- Ensuring that residents are reimbursed for costs or losses that may not be covered by their insurance.
- Providing additional immediate financial assistance, in the form of cash disbursements, to residents in the affected area.
- Reimbursing the City of San Bruno for costs incurred to respond to the incident and to rebuild or repair public infrastructure and facilities.[14]

Funds for losses due to death and personal injury were considered separately.

The administration of the funds for losses related to property damage and community impact would be conducted as a partnership with "government officials, community leaders and organizations, including the American Red Cross and the United Way of the Bay Area," and residents in the affected area would receive "disbursements of $15,000, $25,000, or $50,000 per household depending on the

---

12 CBS SF BayArea, 2010.

13 Pacific Gas and Electric, 2010b.

14 Pacific Gas and Electric, 2010b.

extent of damage incurred." Notably, residents would not be "asked to waive any potential claims in order to receive these funds," which would be "in addition" to money provided to those needing "access to temporary housing and other basic necessities." One immediate use of the fund at the time of the announcement was to present the City of San Bruno with "an initial check for $3 million to help compensate the city for its estimated expenses incurred to date."

PG&E ended its regular staffing of the Recovery Center in late October, shifting toward an approach that would take claims for property damage or loss via the post, fax, or e-mail. But a far more expansive form of assistance was associated with PG&E's Rebuild or Purchase Program, offered to those whose homes were either destroyed or significantly damaged. The utility would either provide funds to those homeowners to rebuild their home in its current location (essentially covering the difference between any homeowner insurance payments and the actual cost of the reconstruction) or buy the property outright. The Value Assurance Program was also set up to guarantee that if someone sold their home within a five-year period beginning January 10, 2011, the utility would pay any difference between the sale price and what PG&E believed to be the property's fair market value, absent "any real or perceived devaluation related to the September 9, 2010 accident."[15] And to help in the recovery of parts of the community affected by the incident but not sustaining significant damage, PG&E's Neighborhood Restoration Plan would reimburse homeowners or pay their contractors up to $10,000 for exterior home improvements or landscaping not covered by insurance and not related to the pipeline explosion. Interestingly, the mayor of San Bruno was critical of the purchase component of the Rebuild or Purchase Program when it was announced, arguing that it would encourage residents to leave the community and jeopardize the rebuilding process. He was also

[15] Public Version: Coordinated Remedies Brief of Pacific Gas and Electric Company, fn. 205, filed May 24, 2013, in *Order Instituting Investigation on the Commission's Own Motion into the Operations and Practices of Pacific Gas and Electric Company*, Investigation Nos. 11-02-016, 11-11-009, and 12-01-007, Pub. Util. Comm'n of the State of California.

displeased with the idea of having "money being presented to people who may still be traumatized by the event."[16]

By May 2011, 28 residents had decided to participate in the Rebuild or Purchase Program, with 21 opting to rebuild while the other seven engaged in negotiations with the utility over the sale price. By the one-year anniversary of the explosion, however, relationships between PG&E and at least some affected homeowners began to sour, even though 24 of the 38 families whose homes were destroyed were rebuilding with PG&E financial assistance, and the other 14 had accepted buyouts ranging from $450,000 to $780,000 or were considering whether to do so. Some complained that PG&E was balking at paying the full price of rebuilding, reportedly due to additional expenses associated with upgraded building codes. Others cited lengthy delays in receiving a buyout offer and disagreements with PG&E's appraisers. (In such instances, the homeowners would have to hire their own appraisers for a second opinion). At the time, PG&E asserted that it would hire mediators to settle any disputes over valuation. Another source of ill will involved PG&E's original promise to "make you whole" in light of the sometimes modest benefits available from homeowners policies and the costs believed to be actually needed to fully replace all that had been lost.[17]

By January 2012, PG&E reported that it had established a trust of up to $70 million for the City of San Bruno to cover the city's fire-related costs (including $1.7 million in outstanding claims by the city), presumably on top of the $3 million disbursement made to the city within a week of the incident. They also indicated that $45 million of the $100 million Rebuild San Bruno Fund had been spent, including a $12 million initial payment to the City of San Bruno trust (arguably a shift of assistance from one fund to another) and $9.3 million in reimbursements to various government agencies. Another $8.5 million in relief checks and gift cards were issued in the immediate aftermath

---

16 Silverfarb, 2010.

17 One example cited at the time involved treasured family photos, for which the insurers were offering only 25 cents each, and, presumably, PG&E was not willing to make up any perceived difference.

of the incident, $7.9 million was paid directly to compensate for property damage or cover gaps in insurance payments, and $850,000 in emergency-assistance payments were made. The programs to address destroyed or severely damaged homes (Rebuild or Purchase), cover shortfalls in fair market value when area homes were sold (Value Assurance), and beautify and improve homes in the affected area that did not suffer significant property damage (Neighborhood Restoration) spent $3.9 million, $470 thousand, and $2.2 million respectively. At the time, PG&E also touted its $1 million contribution to the American Red Cross and again noted that assistance from the Rebuild San Bruno Fund had "been given without any conditions that would restrict recipients from making legal claims against the company for liability and damages" and that the expenditures reported did not include "money spent for personal injuries or litigation."[18]

Legal Developments

Within weeks of the explosion, PG&E began to be hit with litigation initiated by victims in the neighborhood affected by the disaster.[19] Ultimately, over 180 cases involving approximately 500 plaintiffs were filed, including claims for wrongful death, personal injury, property damage, nuisance, and emotional distress. One of the utility's July 2011 court filings in response to these cases attracted considerable attention outside the courthouse and triggered a brief controversy.[20] Its "master answer" recited a number of standard denials of responsibility commonly advanced by defendants in early stages of litigation, including assertions that the plaintiffs' losses and injuries were caused,

---

18 Pacific Gas and Electric, 2012.

19 The description of the legal history surrounding this incident was derived from the following sources: Brooks, 2015; Bulwa, 2012; California Public Utilities Commission, 2015; Dudnick and Lamb, 2016; Morris, 2018; Nemec, 2015; Pacific Gas and Electric, 2016; Pickoff-White, Marks, and Emslie, 2017; Riddle, 2016; Silverfarb, 2010; Van Derbeken, 2011; and complaints and other pleadings and papers filed in related lawsuits.

20 Defendants Pacific Gas and Electric Company and PG&E Corporation's Master Answer to Plaintiffs' Unverified Master Complaint, filed July 5, 2011, in *PG&E "San Bruno Fire" Cases*, Judicial Council Coordination Proceedings No. 4648 (Cal. Super. Ct., San Mateo County).

in whole or in part, by third parties[21] or by the plaintiffs themselves.[22] The master answer also stated the defendant's belief that the plaintiffs' claims were barred, in whole or in part, for two reasons: because the half-century-old pipeline and PG&E's actions before and after the incident were "state-of-the-art" and in compliance with applicable regulations,[23] and because the plaintiffs had already received compensation or assistance for their losses.[24] After media articles reported the reactions of victims and their attorneys to these pleadings, PG&E quickly filed an amended master answer that stated its intention "to make absolutely clear that PG&E does not blame the Plaintiffs and residents who have been affected by this terrible accident and to specifically restate its long-held position that none of the Plaintiffs or residents of San Bruno are at fault. The funds provided to the Plaintiffs and residents immediately after the accident were given with no strings attached and PG&E will not be seeking reimbursement."[25] However, if lawsuits were filed, it seems plausible that previous payments would be deducted from any award or settlement resulting from the suit.

In December 2011, PG&E formally admitted its liability for the incident, reportedly in response to pressure from the judge overseeing victim lawsuits that that been consolidated for pretrial processing in

---

[21] "[B]y unforeseeable, intervening and/or superseding acts of persons or entities other than answering defendants."

[22] "[B]y persons or entities, other than answering defendants, who may have been legally responsible under the doctrine of comparative negligence, contributory negligence, or otherwise at fault, for which the law provides apportionment of fault, reduction, off-set, indemnification or contribution."

[23] "[B]ecause materials and matters alleged and complained about in the Complaint were consistent with available technological, scientific and industrial state-of-the art and in compliance with applicable regulations, and alternative product or facility design was not feasible or practical."

[24] "[B]y accord and satisfaction, payment and release, or estoppel."

[25] Defendants Pacific Gas and Electric Company and PG&E Corporation's Amended Master Answer to Plaintiffs' Unverified Master Complaint, filed July 12, 2011, in *PG&E "San Bruno Fire" Cases*, Judicial Council Coordination Proceedings No. 4648 A (Cal. Super. Ct., San Mateo County).

San Mateo County Superior Court.[26] Reportedly, lawyers for some of the plaintiffs suing the utility claimed that the admission was simply a strategic ploy to reduce the potential for punitive damage awards.

None of the litigation triggered by private parties ever went to trial. Confidential settlements were reached in individual cases at various times in the early years after the explosion, but an October 2012 decision against PG&E on its motion to prevent a jury from considering claims for punitive damages and a looming trial date set for 2013 provided the impetus for negotiating agreements in essentially all of the remaining cases. Encouraged by the state court judge overseeing the consolidated litigation to resolve outstanding matters before trial, counsel reportedly used earlier settlements as benchmarks for creating what was described as a global settlement process for expediting resolution. As a result, "settlement of virtually all of the cases was reached by the third anniversary of the explosion."[27] Though the terms of most of the settlements were never disclosed, PG&E's 2015 annual report to its shareholders reported that the utility had paid $558 million for third-party claims and incurred $92 million in legal costs.

Wrapping up the outstanding tort suits did not end PG&E's legal troubles. In August of 2014, criminal charges were filed in federal court, alleging that the utility had obstructed the National Transportation Safety Board's investigation into the incident and violated various record-keeping, evaluation, and testing provisions of the federal Natural Gas Pipeline Safety Act. Prosecutors sought as much as $562 million in fines and other sanctions, but when the case went to trial two years later, following the dismissal of some of the allegations, PG&E was convicted only on six of the original counts. The sentence included a fine of $3 million (the maximum allowed by law) and five years of probation. In addition, PG&E was ordered to air about $3 million dollars of television advertising (estimated to result in more than 12,000 commercials) describing "the nature of the offenses committed, the convictions, the nature of the punishment imposed, and the steps that will be taken to

---

26 Van Derbeken, 2011.

27 Riddle, 2016.

prevent the recurrence of similar offenses."[28] Similar announcements would be made in full-page ads in the *Wall Street Journal* and *San Francisco Chronicle.* PG&E was also required to perform 10,000 hours of community service, with at least 2,000 of those hours to be performed by "high-level" company personnel.

A potentially more serious problem for the company began with the launch of three separate investigations by the California Public Utility Commission (CPUC) in 2011 and 2012. The enforcement activities focused on the relationship between the San Bruno incident and PG&E's safety-record-keeping, natural gas transmission-pipeline system operations, pipeline installations, integrity management, and other conduct. In May 2013 the proceedings had reached the point where CPUC's consumer protection and safety division issued recommendations to sanction PG&E with a $2.25 billion penalty.[29] One argument in PG&E's brief responding to the recommendation was that the Public Utilities Code requires the CPUC to account for various factors when determining penalties for violating state laws that involve safety standards for pipeline facilities or the transportation of gas. Once such factor would be the "good faith of the utility in attempting to achieve compliance (including the conduct of the utility before, during and after the offense to prevent, detect, disclose and rectify a violation)."[30] To support its assertion that the company's conduct after the accident was indeed performed in good faith, PG&E described the financial assistance that it had provided the City of San Bruno, its reimbursements to local governments for first responder activities, the efforts of its employees to assist victims at the outreach center, and

---

[28] Judgment in a Criminal Case, issued January 31, 2017, in *U.S. v. Pacific Gas and Electric Company*, Case No. 3:14-cr-00175 (U .S. District Court, N.D. Cal.).

[29] Opening Brief of the Consumer Protection and Safety Division on Fines and Remedies, filed May 6, 2013, in *Order Instituting Investigation on the Commission's Own Motion into the Operations and Practices of Pacific Gas and Electric Company*, Investigation Nos. 11-02-016, 11-11-009, and 12-01-007, Pub. Util. Comm'n of the State of California.

[30] Public Version: Coordinated Remedies Brief of Pacific Gas and Electric Company, p. 3, filed May 24, 2013, in *Order Instituting Investigation on the Commission's Own Motion into the Operations and Practices of Pacific Gas and Electric Company*, Investigation Nos. 11-02-016, 11-11-009, and 12-01-007, Pub. Util. Comm'n of the State of California.

the $55 million in immediate and long-term assistance it had given to local victims (such as through relief checks, the Rebuild or Purchase Program, the Neighborhood Restoration Program, property damage payments, etc.). The utility reported that it "took these actions from its sense of responsibility, not in response to Commission directives or any other mandate," and "the record demonstrates that PG&E took these steps, and continues taking them, out of an earnest desire to help make better a tragic situation."

In September 2014, CPUC administrative law judges (ALJs) issued their decision on the investigations, imposing sanctions on PG&E that would include fines and disallowances totaling $1.4 billion. One discussion in the ALJs' decision revolved around PG&E's assertion that its actions to help remediate the effects of the disaster were evidence of good faith and should factor into any penalties. Though the ALJs acknowledged "PG&E's effort immediately after the San Bruno explosion when it provided assistance to the city and its residents affected by the explosion," they did not "find that PG&E . . . acted in good faith to discover, disclose and remedy the violations."[31] In April 2015, the ALJ penalty was independently increased by the Commission to $1.6 billion.

Discussion

While media reports evidence deep dissatisfaction by local elected officials and many affected residents with PG&E's response, two noteworthy points should be mentioned. First, absent PG&E's aggressive efforts to provide funds to rebuild or sell in a manner that would be acceptable to property damage victims, there would have been little recourse for such victims (outside of relying on their own insurance) other than engaging in formal litigation and possibly waiting years before realizing any satisfactory remediation. Instead, residents with destroyed

[31] Presiding Officers' Decision on Fines and Remedies to Be Imposed on Pacific Gas and Electric Company for Specific Violations in Connection with the Operation and Practices of Its Natural Gas Transmission System Pipelines, p. 58, issued September 2, 2014, in *Order Instituting Investigation on the Commission's Own Motion into the Operations and Practices of Pacific Gas and Electric Company*, Investigation Nos. 11-02-016, 11-11-009, and 12-01-007, Pub. Util. Comm'n of the State of California.

homes were at least on their way to having that aspect remedied even before the first anniversary of the fire.

The second point involves PG&E's repeated assurances to the community that whatever assistance was being offered would not prevent the claimant from pursuing traditional litigation strategies in the future (e.g., aid would be "given without any conditions that would restrict recipients from making legal claims against the company for liability and damages"). While there is considerable wiggle room in such announcements, which allows any future recovery efforts to be offset by those already taken, the lack of a formal release requirement probably helped keep the plaintiffs' bar from claiming that the utility had tossed out crumbs to vulnerable victims in hopes it would get them to sign their rights away.

It is also interesting to note that there is no clear evidence that the early assistance efforts carried any weight in the ALJs' calculation of award size. The $2.25 billion penalty initially proposed by the CPUC consumer protection and safety division was reduced to $1.4 billion, with the ALJs acknowledging PG&E's early assistance efforts. It is unclear how much, if any, the penalty was reduced due to PG&E's early assistance efforts. In addition, it could be that other aspects of PG&E's behavior were considered so egregious that they overwhelmed whatever good was accomplished through early assistance.

Example 3: Arkema Organic Peroxide Combustion

The Incident and Aftermath

On August 12, 2017, the National Weather Service (NWS) Hurricane Center issued a "Tropical Weather Outlook" statement reporting that a tropical wave, which had just emerged off the west coast of Africa, was forecast "to move westward over the next couple of days" but had a low chance of forming into a tropical cyclone in the near term.[32] Five days later, the disturbance had morphed into a tropical storm designated as Harvey, but then it began to die out. Its remnants, disorganized

---

32 National Weather Service, 2017a.

showers and thunderstorms, drifted westward over the Caribbean Sea and toward the Yucatan Peninsula.[33] Reaching the southwestern Gulf of Mexico, the disturbance redeveloped into a tropical depression and then a tropical storm. On August 24, it was upgraded by the NWS to hurricane status and was moving north-northwest toward Texas.[34] At that point, the NWS began to warn of "life-threatening and devastating flooding expected near the coast due to heavy rainfall and storm surge," but when the eyewall of Harvey finally made landfall by late evening on Friday, August 25, it was a Category 4 hurricane, and the flooding potential was described as "catastrophic" given potential "rain accumulations of 15 to 30 inches and isolated maximum amounts of 40 inches over the middle and upper Texas coast through next Wednesday."[35] When Harvey disappeared about eight days after landfall, 51.88 inches of rain had been recorded at a weather station along the Cedar Bayou, east of Houston, a record amount for any single storm in the continental United States.[36]

On the day that Harvey was classified as a hurricane, workers at Arkema Inc.'s Crosby chemical plant (located just 8 miles north of the Cedar Bayou rain gauge) were preparing for the threatening storm.[37] Local weather forecasts were predicting 15 to 18 inches of rain in the area, enough water to close roads in the vicinity of the plant; however, plant personnel believed that the potentially higher amounts of precipitation the NWS reports warned of would trigger no more than about 2 ft of floodwater. The next day, the severity of the forecasts had increased markedly, prompting Arkema to send most of the plant's employees home but to retain a 12-member "ride-out" team to monitor

---

[33] National Weather Service, 2017b.

[34] National Weather Service, 2017c; National Weather Service, 2017d.

[35] National Weather Service, 2017e; National Weather Service, 2017f.

[36] Meyer, 2017.

[37] The description of events surrounding this incident was derived from the following sources: Arkema, Inc., 2017a; Arkema, Inc., 2017b; Arkema, Inc., 2017c; Arkema, Inc., 2017d; Arkema, Inc., 2017e; Dempsey, Blakinger, and Ellis, 2017; Feuk, 2017; Horton, Wang, and Bever, 2017; KHOU, 2017; Society of the Plastics Industry, Inc., 2013; Stuckey, 2018; Trevizo, 2019; and U.S. Chemical Safety and Hazard Investigation Board, 2018.

the situation at the plant and to address any issues until the storm had passed. Despite the worsening conditions, Arkema staff believed the plant's electrical systems (including backup power capabilities) would hold up through the storm.

The power situation was of particular concern at the plant because the facility's main purpose was to produce organic peroxides, a family of chemicals that are vital to the plastic and rubber industries. Depending on their composition, organic peroxides can be fire and explosion hazards as well as extremely toxic or corrosive, potentially causing irritation of the skin and eyes and, in some instances, liver damage. Many varieties of organic peroxides are classified by their self-accelerating decomposition temperature (SADT), above which a chemical process leading to an explosion will begin. In order to maintain organic peroxides at temperatures far enough below the SADT to allow for safe handling and storage, manufacturers and users of the chemicals must employ commercial-grade refrigeration systems. Reliable sources of electrical power are a necessary requirement for such systems.

On Saturday, August 26, enough rain had fallen in the greater Houston area to cause the water levels in Cedar Bayou to raise about 6 feet above the top of the bank. Located within the Cedar Bayou watershed, the plant then began to experience flooding, raising concerns that power might have to be turned off at various facilities on the property to avoid short-circuiting. The flooding significantly worsened on Sunday with parts of the property now under 4 feet of water. The plan was to move the chemicals from refrigerated warehouses threatened by flooding (and a subsequent loss of power) to others on the property that were in more secure locations and, if necessary, to a group of refrigerated truck trailers that were normally used as surplus storage on the site. By that evening all of the warehouses save one had lost their ability to cool the organic peroxides due to rising waters, so their contents were transferred to some of the trailers. When each trailer was sufficiently full, it was moved to a section of the facility that was on somewhat higher ground.

Despite a break in the rain in the early hours of Monday, August 28, water levels continued to rise to the point where forklifts were no longer operational, and, as a result, the team had to move

2,000 pounds of chemicals by hand from the last refrigerated warehouse (its power having been turned off hours before) to three nearby trailers. By the time the work was complete, these vehicles were no longer able to be relocated to higher ground because water levels had also compromised the electrical systems of the semi-tractor trucks used for moving the trailers. The team's hope was that the self-powered refrigeration units on the three trailers would continue to operate until the flood waters receded. Unfortunately, those hopes were dashed when, on the morning of Tuesday, the twenty-ninth, the team found that one of the three trailers had partially tipped over during the night, possibly from strong floodwater currents. This discovery strongly suggested that the refrigeration units in one or more of the three trailers were likely to fail at some point. Given the implications of such a scenario, corporate management requested that local emergency responders evacuate the ride-out team by boat.

Based on information that the departed workers and Arkema management provided about the potential for explosion and fire from the decomposing organic peroxides, local authorities initiated an evacuation of residences within a 1.5-mile radius of the plant, ultimately moving approximately 200 residents out of the area and shutting down U.S. Highway 90, which ran adjacent to the site. An estimated 350 homes were within the evacuation zone. The evacuation was not as smooth as one might hope. Some residents reported learning about the orders to leave not through knocks on their door or official announcements but through friends or social media. A robocall system, which a previous legal action had required Arkema to employ for alerting those in the vicinity of any pollutant leakages that would have potentially adverse health or safety impacts, was apparently not triggered, although no known releases of the organic peroxides had taken place by this point.

The public statements Arkema issued on Wednesday certainly did not underplay the potential for danger. After apologizing "to everyone impacted by our situation, particularly in combination with the horrible conditions visited upon the region by the hurricane," the company's CEO announced that the plant had "lost critical refrigeration of the materials on site that could now explode and cause a subsequent intense fire" and that the "high water and lack of power leave us with no way to prevent it."[38] At the time, Arkema also announced that they were setting up a hotline to handle questions from the public (which was maintained through December) as well as a walk-in center to handle financial claims and offer various forms of assistance.

Later that night, police officers traveling on Highway 90 reported that they had encountered an irritating white smoke over the road. Other first responders in the early hours of Thursday also reported white smoke and symptoms that suggested exposure to noxious chemicals (ultimately, 15 first responders would be treated for respiratory irritation). At about 2 a.m. on Thursday, the tipped trailer finally caught fire. An Arkema executive stated at the time that the company fully expected "that the eight other containers will do the same thing," noting that Arkema officials "anticipate that all of this product is going to degrade; we don't know exactly how long that's going to take . . . whether it's today, tomorrow, we just don't know; it's impossible to predict."[39] On Friday, September 1, the two other trailers that had not been moved also caught fire, sending plumes of black smoke high into the air. The next day, aerial reconnaissance flights revealed that at least one of the trailers sitting on high ground had lost its refrigeration capacity and that there was material outside the trailers suspected to be decomposing organic peroxides.

The situation with displaced residents seemed to be degrading as well. Arkema established an Assistance Center at a local high school on Saturday (which would remain open for almost another two weeks) and handed out hotel vouchers and cash to cover some expenses of the affected locals, but the distribution was running into problems. Some evacuees told local reporters that they had waited in line for hours, only to be told to return the next day. There was also frustration over the fact that no definitive estimate could be given of when access to the cordoned-off area would be permitted. And while hotel vouchers could be obtained, there were no rooms available locally, so voucher holders

---

[38] Arkema, Inc., 2017a.

[39] Horton, Wang, and Bever, 2017.

would have to travel to Houston or other cities to actually find a place to stay. One resident whose home was about a quarter of a mile from the plant reportedly was tired of the lack of communication about temporary housing, about when the evacuation would be lifted, and about the potential danger from explosions: "At first, I was understanding; it was an accident. . . . But now, they're jerking us around."[40] Despite the complaints, Arkema asserted two days later that the company had "helped over 100 families find housing since getting on site" and had assisted "with transportation, with essentially all that you can imagine, getting their lives back to normal."[41]

With evacuated residents increasingly displeased about being blocked from returning to their homes and reportedly pressuring officials to find some sort of solution, a joint command group (consisting of the Harris County Fire Marshal's Office, Pollution Control Services department, and Sheriff's Office and Constables; the Crosby Volunteer Fire Department; the federal Environmental Protection Agency (EPA); Arkema; and other agencies) decided to conduct a controlled burn of the remaining trailers Sunday afternoon. By that evening the burn had been completed and air-monitoring within the evacuation zone indicated that there were no peroxide readings above baseline levels. So in the early hours of Monday, September 4, the evacuation ended. Arkema announced that day that if residents in the area found debris or ash on their property, they could call the call center, and a team would be sent out for its removal. One concern of evacuees was the condition of the livestock and pets that they had left behind and that had gone without care for nearly a week; there were reports of returning residents finding dead animals on their properties.

In early October the company noted that, in response to the incident, it had "served hundreds of families, arranging hotel rooms and rental cars, and giving them more than $100,000 in cash and gift cards for immediate needs such as food, clothing, medicine or pet care," and

40 Dempsey, Blakinger, and Ellis, 2017.

41 Feuk, 2017.

had taken in "hundreds" of claims for nonflood related damage.[42] The company asserted that "more than 70 percent of homeowners who have filed claims have had an initial [property inspection] to start the processing of their claims" and that in a "limited number of cases we have already paid claims, though typically the process takes longer." However, Arkema appeared to suggest that at least some of the delay was due to the need for "supporting documentation such as receipts for expenses, and estimates or invoices from service providers," though "fewer than one percent" of claiming residents had "submitted estimates of the cost of repair" so far. It also touted the fact that it had donated $500,000 to charities addressing Hurricane Harvey-related needs.

Legal Developments

Within a week after the evacuation orders lifted, the first civil lawsuit against Arkema was filed in Harris County District Court on behalf of individually named area residents as well as a number of first responders.[43] The matter was quickly removed by Arkema to the Federal District Court for the Southern District of Texas, and in that venue more residents and first responders were added as plaintiffs. The suit alleged personal injuries, loss of future earning capacity, mental anguish, a need for ongoing medical monitoring, various consequential damages (such as the costs of travel, alternative living arrangements, and cleanup), real and personal property damage, and financial injuries to businesses.

A second case was filed less than a month later in federal district court.[44] Instead of naming individual plaintiffs, the suit sought class action status in which 15 representative plaintiffs would stand in for similarly situated residents (including those outside the evacuation zone) and first responders. A key allegation of this case was that post-

---

[42] Arkema, Inc., 2017d.

[43] The description of the legal history surrounding this incident was derived from the following sources: Blakinger, 2018; Dempsey and Blakinger, 2017; Kuzydym and Noll, 2017; Oberg, 2017; Ortiz, 2018; Spinelli, 2018; Stuckey, 2018; Whitfield, 2018; and complaints and other pleadings and papers filed in related lawsuits.

[44] Kuzydym and Noll, 2017.

evacuation testing of off-site ash, soil, and dust samples indicated the presence of toxic substances that were asserted to have come from the clouds of smoke generated by the fires at the plant. Another was that residents and first responders breathed air contaminated with chemicals originating from the plant or had contact with contaminated flood waters. Compensation for personal injury, emotional distress, property damage, and loss of income was sought as well as a punitive damage award, plus changes in Arkema's pollution-control policies, improved measures to maintain continuous power, modifications to the plant's community warning plans, the replacement of contaminated topsoil, and medical monitoring.

In November 2017, Harris County and the Texas Commission on Environmental Quality (TCEQ) initiated a civil action against Arkema in Harris County District Court that sought various civil penalties of up to $1 million, the costs of responding to the incident (estimated to be at least $44,000) and a third-party audit of Arkema's disaster-response plans and its Crosby plant operations.

In March 2018, Liberty County (located east of Crosby) initiated its own civil action against Arkema in Liberty County District Court (TCEQ was a plaintiff as well). To represent its interests, the county hired the attorney who was one of the counsel representing plaintiffs in the initial lawsuit, filed the previous September. A particular focus of this litigation was the impact of wastewater tanks filling with rainwater, overflowing into containment dikes that, in turn, combined with floodwaters that reached Liberty County. The suit alleged that Arkema had violated the Texas Clean Air Act, the Texas Water Code, and various health and safety codes, as well as creating a public nuisance. In addition to seeking fines, the suit demanded that Arkema clean up any residual contamination in Liberty County.

But perhaps the most closely watched legal action connected to the incident began with an indictment handed down by a Harris County grand jury in August 2018, charging Arkema, the chief executive officer of its North American operations, and the Crosby plant manager with criminal conduct, potentially resulting in a sentence of up to five years in prison for the two employees and corporate fines of up to $1 million. In April 2019, another Harris County grand jury indicted the company and its vice president for logistics on felony assault charges, alleging that the defendants had falsely informed emergency management officials that Arkema had real-time data monitoring of the site's storage facilities. While a number of other industrial operations in Texas have been sued regarding their conduct during Hurricane Harvey, it appears that, as this paper is written, these indictments have been the only instances in which corporate employees have been accused of criminal conduct in regard to Harvey-related environmental issues. One environmental law professor noted that the prosecution triggered "a lot of interest, a lot of attention, a lot of concern" for industrial operators because it "creates the possibility that even companies that think that they've gotten their compliance in a row and they're complying with regulations may still face possible criminal liability if they are deemed to (have) acted in a reckless fashion, which isn't really defined by a particular statutory requirement."[45]

As of the writing of this paper, trial in the criminal cases had not yet begun, and the suits brought by Harris and Liberty counties do not appear to have concluded. The first civil case against Arkema (the one involving individually named plaintiffs) was stayed by the judge in October 2018 until the conclusion of the criminal prosecutions, though in August 2019 the plaintiffs added a Texas defendant to the case, which triggered a remand to Harris County District Court for all further proceedings. In June 2019, the judge overseeing the putative class action filed in federal district court also stayed that matter until the criminal cases were resolved.

Discussion

Unlike the other incidents in this chapter, the event that directly triggered the initial harm was not sudden or unexpected. Decomposition and subsequent ignition of the contents of one of the storage trailers that occurred late Wednesday, the twenty-ninth, had been anticipated since the previous morning when the ride-out team noticed that the vehicle had partially tipped over. Even before that point, on Monday

---

[45] Ortiz, 2018.

afternoon, it had been clear that three refrigerated trailers being used as backup storage could not be moved out of the rising floodwaters because the plant's semi-tractor trucks had stalled; as a result, it was just a matter of time before the situation would degrade catastrophically. In many ways, the Arkema incident was marked by waiting: waiting for the initial combustion of the first trailer, waiting for the two other backup storage trailers in low-lying areas to combust as well, waiting to see what might happen with the trailers on high ground that were beginning to fail, and waiting for the evacuation orders to be lifted. The uncertainty might have contributed to some of the discontent voiced by area residents, who had been forced to leave their homes in a hurry during the landfall of Harvey, which was already a stressful time. As one evacuee later noted,

> For a while, we weren't really sure what we were supposed to be worried about—explosions or smoke—and we thought the evacuation would last for a day or so; we didn't realize it would be almost a week.[46]

Another issue that came up was the quality of information people were receiving. While the company attempted to communicate with the public through media statements, press releases, Twitter tweets, Facebook posts, and its company website, some of the information being provided was reportedly "ambiguous."[47] It might have been mostly one-way as well, as questions from community members posted on the company's Facebook page (where the latest announcements about the situation at the plant could be found) were said to have received no public response from the chemical manufacturer.

Given the ongoing confusion and uncertainty surrounding the event, Arkema's assistance efforts as the incident was unfolding may not have been perceived as a completely generous and altruistic exercise in good will. Lengthy waits at the Assistance Center would not have helped in this regard, especially for those who were eventually told to

---

[46] Feuk, 2017.

[47] Stuckey, 2018.

come back the next day or for those given hotel vouchers that were essentially worthless if they needed to remain in or around Crosby. Some of the problems were clearly not of Arkema's making. For example, Harvey had resulted in an unprecedented demand on lodging in southeast Texas, the company was unable to assess the situation at the plant from the ground, there were weather-related transportation difficulties in delivering aid or deploying company assets, the usual channels of communicating with the community had broken down (many in the region were without power, phone service, cable television, or the internet), and the availability of first responders and disaster-related resources were severely reduced due to the regional emergency (e.g., it does not appear that the Red Cross ever deployed to Crosby). Nevertheless, the incident serves as an example of how a less-than-successful early assistance program can become a source of dissatisfaction and frustration for a community rather than a universally welcome means for recovery.

Example 4: *Athos I* Oil Spill

Background on the Oil Pollution Act of 1990

The Oil Pollution Act of 1990 (OPA) was enacted in response to the 1989 grounding of the *Exxon Valdez.* Its aim was to create a comprehensive legal framework for adequately addressing the consequences of oil spills in the navigable waters of the United States.[48] OPA is a complex piece of legislation, and its operation and interpretation can be the subject of intense legal debate (particularly in the aftermath of the 2010 *Deepwater Horizon* disaster), but in a nutshell it offers a mechanism for financing the cleanup of discharged oil and for compensating individuals, businesses, and governments that have incurred spill-related damages in a manner that does not necessarily require the

---

48 Oil Pollution Act of 1990, Pub. L. No. 101–380, 104 Stat 484 (1990). See also U.S. Congress, House Committee on Merchant Marine and Fisheries, *Report Accompanying H.R. 1465, Oil Pollution Prevention, Removal, Liability, and Compensation Act of 1989*, H. Rept. 101-242, Part 2, 101st Cong., 1st sess., 1989, p. 31.

utilization of the tort liability system. It should be made clear that traditional civil litigation in the wake of an oil release is certainly possible, even when OPA's mandates apply, and if the incident is a major one, such litigation is arguably an absolute certainty. Nevertheless, the framework provides a means of encouraging companies that are likely to bear some responsibility for the cause of an oil discharge to take rapid steps toward ameliorating its impact on the environment, individuals, businesses, and government agencies.

The post-spill operation of OPA begins with the United States Coast Guard or the EPA identifying a responsible party (RP) based on the source of the oil.[49] An RP might be the owners of a vessel, the operator of an onshore refinery or a pipeline, or the licensee of an offshore oil lease. It is the oil's source, and not the underlying cause of the discharge, that is the basis of the initial RP designation. The RP would then be liable for any costs incurred by federal, state, or local governments for removal of the oil; damage to natural resources; first responder expenses; damage to real or personal property; loss of the use of natural resources by those who depend on them for food, economic security, or other products; and lost profits or diminished earnings capacity. With the exceptions of damage related to personal injuries and deaths (which are not included within the OPA framework), the types of claims that may be advanced against an RP mirror or even exceed those that might be brought against a defendant in a civil tort action.[50]

The person or entity identified as an RP can shed that designation if it can be established that the discharge was solely caused by the acts or omissions of a third party without any contractual relationship to the RP.

---

[49] The general description of OPA's provisions presented here is based on Chapter Five in Pace and Dixon, 2017.

[50] OPA allows for the recovery of "pure economic loss," in which a claimant seeks compensation for financial losses (such as lost profits or earnings) even though there was neither physical or mental injuries to the claimant nor physically damaged property. An example would be a commercial fishing company claiming reduced income because of adverse publicity over the condition of fish in affected waters after a spill, even though the oil did not directly affect the company's fleet, its personnel, or marine life. Such a claim would not be permitted under traditional tort law.

The shift of the designation can take place only if the RP had exercised all due care in handling the oil and taken precautions against the foreseeable acts or omissions of others. Until that showing is made, the RP must continue to fulfill its cleanup responsibilities and continue to process damage claims. A discharge that was shown to be the sole result of an act of God or war would also relieve the RP from liability.

Designation of an RP can take place within hours after a spill has been discovered. Unless the RP formally denies the identification (perhaps by asserting the third-party defense described previously), it is supposed to publicly advertise its status as an RP and announce instructions on how claims should be presented. Any such claims received are handled administratively by the RP, and a 90-day limit is placed on the consideration of submitted demands. Typically, a claim against an RP is straightforward enough that those believing they have been damaged do not require assistance of counsel to submit the necessary paperwork and supporting documentation.

In instances where the RP fails to advertise and implement a claims process or where a claimant is unsatisfied with the outcome of its dealings with the RP, the United States will essentially stand in the RP's shoes. Those damaged economically or in some other way by the spill can then file a claim with the Coast Guard's National Pollution Funds Center (NPFC). Claims are considered under essentially the same criteria that an RP would (or should) apply, and if the request is deemed appropriate, the NPFC will pay the claims using funds from the Oil Spill Liability Trust Fund (OSLTF). The OSLTF is financed by a tax on crude oil that is either used in or exported from the United States and by previous recoveries for natural resource damages, subrogation actions, and penalty assessments. Any such payments to claimants out of the OSLTF then give the United States subrogation rights to proceed against the RP to recover those expenditures plus interest, administrative and adjudicative costs (such as those incurred in considering claims from third parties), and attorneys' fees. The OSLTF is also used to pay for cleanup and remediation efforts undertaken by government agencies and private parties when the RP is unwilling or unable to do so, thus allowing for a rapid response without waiting for a financial commitment from an RP. The OSLTF is also the source of funding for addressing the consequences of oil spills in which the source of the oil (or the identity of the owner of the source) cannot be determined (designated as a "mystery spill").

OPA is notable in that it requires claimants to use the RP's claim process if one was set up appropriately and in a timely manner after the EPA's or Coast Guard's identification of the RP. Only after that process has been completed can the claimant choose to proceed against the OSLTF or file a civil action against the RP to recover its losses. So at least in theory, OPA provides for an initial administrative alternative to traditional tort litigation.

While RPs can challenge the original identification of its status as a responsible party (asserting, for example, that the spill was the result of an unforeseeable act of terrorism), they often have considerable incentive not to do so. Legislation creating OPA followed the long-standing tradition of maritime law in limiting the maximum liability of vessels for damage claims and the costs of removal and remediation and extended those liability caps to other sources of oil, such as drilling platforms and onshore storage facilities. The size of these limitations varies by the type and size of the source (ultralarge crude carriers, mobile offshore drilling units, tugboats, refineries, and harbor fuel docks all have different caps), but they offer considerable financial protection as long as the proximate cause of the incident was not RP behavior constituting gross negligence, willful misconduct, or violation of an applicable federal safety, construction, or operating regulation. In instances where the RP's OPA-related expenditures have reached the liability threshold, it need no longer pay any additional claims. Those seeking damages for their losses after the cap has been reached are not without recourse, however, as they can file a claim with the NPFC and be paid out of the trust fund.

Because OPA is administered by multiple government agencies and because there is no single-point source for collecting data for all oil spills, identifying the number of instances annually where OPA's provisions would be triggered in the aftermath of a discharge is problematic. But based on information from a number of sources, a reasonable estimate might be that in 2015, there were about 3,000 oil-spill incidents with at least the potential for an RP to be identified.[51] Relatively few of these incidents received attention from news media or anyone not directly connected with the spill or its aftermath, as presumably OPA's provisions worked both quietly and as intended in the vast majority of spills: RPs rapidly addressing their responsibilities to clean up and remediate the immediate effects of the discharge and providing a streamlined administrative process for considering claims from those whose property and financial interests were impaired (and when that does not happen, having the NPFC step in). Something to remember is that no provisions in OPA force an RP to take overt steps to cover the costs of addressing an oil spill; indeed, many RPs choose to do nothing at all in response to the EPA's or Coast Guard's designation, deciding instead to either challenge government subrogation actions, which might not be initiated until years later, or to simply pay NPFC's final bill when it is presented. Because an RP operating within the OPA framework receives claims and cleans up discharges long before any tort litigation has been resolved or any court order issued, we believe it is appropriate to characterize those actions as a type of "encouraged" early assistance. The discussion that follows presents one example of how OPA has worked in practice.

The Incident and Aftermath

On November 26, 2004, the 37,900-gross-tonnage oil tanker T/V *Athos I* was carrying about 14 million gallons of heavy Venezuelan crude oil as it approached the Citgo asphalt refinery on the Delaware River near Paulsboro, New Jersey.[52] The *Athos I* had been chartered by

---

[51] See discussion and figures in Ramseur, 2017, pp. 2–7.

[52] The description of the events surrounding this incident was derived from the following sources: Boyajian, 2016; Memorandum and/or Opinion, entered July 25, 2016, in *United States v. Citgo Asphalt Refining Company*, No. 08-cv-2898 and *In re Petition of Frescati Shipping Company, Ltd.*, No. 05-cv-305 (U.S. District Court, E.D. Pa.); Dakss, 2004; De La Rue and Anderson, 2009; George, 2004; Hajna, 2004; Hajna, 2005; Moran Shipping, 2004; Moran Shipping, 2005; Muldoon, 2007; *The Delaware River Oil Spill: Hearing Before the Subcommittee on Coast Guard and Maritime Transportation of the Committee on Transportation and Infrastructure, House of Representatives, January 18, 2005* (testimony of Rear Admiral Sally Brice-O'Hara); U.S. Coast Guard, 2006; U.S. Commerce Department, 2014.

Citgo for the journey, and the contract to do so contained a standard clause common in such agreements, wherein the charterer would not require the vessel to call at an unsafe port or to enter an unsafe berth. The tanker was owned by Cyprus-based Frescati Shipping but managed by Tsakos Shipping and Trading. (For the purposes of this discussion we refer to both entities collectively as "Frescati.")

The tide was relatively low at the time, but there were no problems noted as a local dock pilot began to guide the vessel into the refinery's berth. To reach the docking area, the *Athos I* would have exited the river's main shipping channel and crossed an area identified as "Federal Anchorage Number Nine," a section of the river that was neither owned nor controlled by Citgo but was the only practical approach to its berth.

Just as the tanker was docking, crews on assisting tugboats noticed an oil slick, and the ship then listed and lost power. The holding tanks affected by the leak were identified and their contents transferred to other sections of the vessel, but not before 263,000 gallons of oil had entered the river. The next day, divers found two gashes in the hull measuring 5 ft and 2 ft long. Subsequent searches of the anchorage's bottom found three relatively large objects, including a 9-ton, 7-ft-long anchor, and testing of paint samples from the objects matched those on the tanker's hull. The anchor was later determined to be the main culprit behind the oil discharge, but the identity of its owner was never confirmed.

A Coast Guard Federal On-Scene Coordinator directed the incident response, and Frescati was designated as the RP. Frescati immediately engaged the services of The O'Brien's Group, an oil-spill management company, to participate in a "unified command" with the Coast Guard and with stakeholders from Pennsylvania, New Jersey, and Delaware. The primary objective of the unified command was to prevent further discharge, assess the condition of the shoreline (tidal currents had carried some of the crude upriver, and the natural flow of the Delaware carried the remainder south), install protective booming, provide updates to the public, and perform other urgent functions. Despite the containment efforts (of which much was performed by contractors hired directly by Frescati), the spill fouled 57 miles of the Delaware River shoreline (with a total shoreline impact that was far greater), closed the river to vessel traffic for a few days, temporarily shut down the busy Port of Philadelphia, affected onshore facilities (especially those dependent upon waterborne deliveries and shipping), damaged critical wetlands and other sensitive environments, killed an estimated 12,000 birds, and prompted an 11-day precautionary shutdown for two reactors at the Salem Nuclear Power Plant in New Jersey.

Frescati's financial expenditures for the cleanup, for third-party claims in the early days after the discharge, and for the implementation of its emergency-spill response plan under the Coast Guard's direction were extensive. Much of the containment activities, including decontamination of other vessels, structures, equipment, and the shoreline, was performed by contractors paid directly by Frescati. Within two days of the spill, the company also hired Hudson Marine Management Services to receive claims for property damage, other losses, and for remediation that individuals or companies had performed by themselves or that others had performed on their behalf. By December 2, about 300 such claims had been filed by owners of small boats, marinas, and docks and by shippers whose vessels were held up while leaving or entering the port. In January of 2005 Frescati estimated that it had incurred about $95 million in remediation and oil-recovery expenses and had received over 650 public and private damage claims by property and boat owners along the river and its tributary wetlands. Primarily, claims alleged problems with oil on docks, beaches, industrial properties, and private boats (private boat owners submitted the majority of claims). Others claimed they lost business as a result of the spill. Eventually, Frescati would assert that it paid out about $180 million in total cleanup costs, claims, and ship damages.

The size of the expenditures incurred in such a short time was an important issue, because under OPA at the time, a vessel of the size and configuration of the *Athos I* had a total limitation of liability on oil-spill-related losses of about $45 million. Frescati had already exceeded that limit within weeks of the spill but continued to make expenditures related to oil recovery and remediation. In March it reached an agreement with the Coast Guard in which the NPFC would handle all unpaid and future claims for property damage, business losses, remaining cleanup costs, and the like.

The move to allow the NPFC to process claims simply changed the identity of the party making the payment; the rules for evaluating claims would be unmodified and, unlike the situation with Frescati's capped liability, the trust fund could theoretically pay out as much as a billion dollars before its OPA-mandated limits on single-incident outlays were reached. Still, some in the affected community were not pleased. One cruise boat owner, who believed that his company had lost $12,000 in reservations, was frustrated about the pace at which claims were being addressed, asserting that the vessel's owners were "spending a lot of money on cleaning up rocks and piers, but I'm just trying to get by," and now there would be "nothing left for the little guy."[53] But, in fact, the NPFC wound up paying out over $160 million in damage claims plus another $48 million in oil-removal costs by 2013.[54]

The OPA limit on liability that Frescati exceeded with its expenditures for remediation and cleanup had an important consequence. Under OPA, as long as Frescati's payments in excess of the liability cap were incurred in order to prevent, minimize, or mitigate the effects of the incident, the vessel's owners would be free to file a claim for reimbursement against the OSLTF, just like any other party. Then in January 2006, the Coast Guard investigation was complete, and its report confirmed that there was no evidence of negligence by the *Athos I* crew, opening the door for Frescati to eventually obtain reimbursement of $88 million of its expenditures in excess of the $45.5 million cap.

Legal Developments

The sole instance of traditional civil litigation we were able to identify, which involved claims brought by third parties against the vessel's owners or operators or against the chartering oil company, was a putative class action originally filed in New Jersey State Court in the first

53 Hajna, 2005.

54 U.S. Government Accountability Office, 2015.

half of 2005, removed to the Federal District Court for the District of New Jersey, and then transferred across the Delaware to the Eastern District of Pennsylvania.[55] The case was brought on behalf of property owners in Camden County, New Jersey, alleging property damage, economic loss, inconvenience, and diminished real estate value as a result of contaminants washing up on their properties. In May 2006 the class action allegations were dismissed, the plaintiffs were encouraged to file their claims with the NPFC or the New Jersey Spill Fund, and the matter administratively closed.

A much more robust line of litigation began in January 2005 and, as this paper is written, is still in play more than 14 years later. This line addresses allocation of liability among PRPs, which is another factor that may enter PRP decisions to offer early assistance. It began when Frescati initiated a relatively routine maritime action that sought to limit the value of damage claims unrelated to oil pollution to the post-accident value of the vessel and its freight (asserted by Frescati to be $5.1 million). From there the action morphed into a vehicle for Frescati to seek reimbursement from Citgo for all of its spill-related expenditures other than the $88 million it had received from the OSLTF.[56] The United States joined the litigation as a plaintiff in order to seek its own reimbursement from Citgo for the OSLTF payments to Frescati in a subrogation action. Frescati first asserted its claim based on contract law, arguing that the safe-berth clause in the chartering agreement meant that the berth owner (Citgo) would be strictly liable if damage occurred without any fault on the part of the vessel. Alternatively, it sought to recover under a tort theory, arguing that Citgo was negligent for failing to discover the anchor in the approach, because a "safe berth" would have included the approach to the jetty and not

[55] The description of the legal history surrounding this incident was derived from the following sources: Adjudication, entered April 12, 2011, in *United States v. Citgo Asphalt Refining Company*, No. 08-cv-2898 and *In re Petition of Frescati Shipping Company, Ltd.*, No. 05-cv-305 (U.S. District Court, E.D. Pa.); Associated Press, 2011; Gallagher, 2016; Waid, 2018; and complaints and other pleadings and papers filed in related lawsuits.

[56] A separate action Frescati brought against Citgo in July 2005 was essentially subsumed into the reimbursement proceeding and dismissed a few months later.

just the area immediately adjacent to the structure. In 2011, after a 41-day bench trial, the judge rejected Frescati's arguments, holding that Citgo had no reason to suspect that the objects were in the water (especially given that 42 vessels had docked at the jetty without incident in 2004) and that, in any event, Citgo had no duty to maintain a common anchorage regularly used by hundreds of vessels that never docked at its jetty. Further, the judge said that to hold otherwise would "have the effect of potentially expanding the definition of 'approach' to the entire Anchorage or to the entire Delaware River."[57] Moreover, under the chartering contract, Citgo had only a duty of due diligence to select a safe berth, and the judge felt that the duty had been exercised appropriately.

The verdict in Citgo's favor was appealed, and in 2013 the federal Court of Appeals for the Third Circuit affirmed some parts of the district court's judgment orders but vacated most of the others and remanded the case for further proceedings. Importantly, it ruled that Frescati was a beneficiary of the safe berth warrant, which was an "express assurance" that the destination port was safe for the *Athos I* in the condition the ship was in at the time the contract was made—a condition in which the vessel drafted 37 ft of water or less.[58] The trial court was ordered to determine whether the arriving draft of the vessel exceeded that amount, what the depth and positioning of the anchor were at the time of the impact, and whether the approach (defined as the path from the ship channel to the berth) was safe.

In 2016 the case was retried by a different judge, and questions raised by the Court of Appeals were addressed with another 31 days of testimony. The outcome was very different this time, with the judge finding that Citgo warranted a safe berth with the understanding that the *Athos I* would be drawing as much as 37 ft of water—and, in fact, the vessel did comply with the limitation only to strike the anchor. The court also found that owners of terminals have a duty to identify

---

[57] Adjudication, entered April 12, 2011, in *United States v. Citgo Asphalt Refining Company*, No. 08-cv-2898 and *In re Petition of Frescati Shipping Company, Ltd.*, No. 05-cv-305 (U.S. District Court, E.D. Pa.).

[58] *In re Frescati Shipping Co., Ltd.*, 718 F.3d 184 (3d Cir. 2013).

imminent dangers to ships during approach, regardless of who owns the approach. As such, Frescati would be entitled $55.5 million in damages. But while the United States was under no obligation to perform depth soundings in the approach, it did so as a matter of routine anyway, and local shipping relied on those measurements. The judge felt that the manner in which the soundings were taken was based on older technology but that, had the United States used state-of-the-art sonar, it would have detected the anchor. As a result, the government's claim against Citgo would be cut in half as a matter of equity, and the United States would receive only $44 million in reimbursement.

Citgo appealed the decision, but in 2018, the Third Circuit upheld the judge's rulings regarding Frescati's claims. Moreover, it held that the equitable recoupment doctrine used to cut the 2016 award to the United States in half was not applicable, because the United States' claims were brought under a subrogation theory; as such, the defense would only be applicable if Citgo could have asserted it against Frescati. Since the vessel owner had nothing to do whatsoever with taking soundings of the Delaware River, the defense was not available, and Citgo would have to repay the entire $88 million. As of this writing, certiorari has been granted by the United States Supreme Court on Citgo's appeal of the 2018 Third Circuit decision.

Discussion

The *Athos I* incident generated surprisingly few lawsuits for an event that was estimated by the Coast Guard to have triggered about one-quarter of a billion dollars in direct expenditures—and for an event that appears to be the third most costly vessel-sourced oil spill in the United States behind *Exxon Valdez* and *Deepwater Horizon* and that led to the passage of the federal Delaware River Protection Act of 2006 (markedly increasing OPA's liability limits, in part, to provide incentives for phasing out single-hulled tankers).[59] OPA certainly does not eliminate civil litigation in the aftermath of an oil spill—the thou-

[59] U.S. Coast Guard, 2018, Attachment A. As a result of the 2006 legislation, a vessel of *Athos I*'s type and size would now have liability limits about three times the size as those in 2004.

sands of cases filed in regard to *Deepwater Horizon* easily dispel that notion—but the law provides at least an option for dealing with high volumes of claims administratively rather than through an adversarial process.[60] That seems to be the case here.

That said, our interest here is not in the degree to which OPA sidesteps the tort system but instead in whether it facilitates efforts to address the needs of a community affected by a disaster, even when the issue of legal causation is far from settled. By that test, OPA "worked" in regard to *Athos I.* It is easy to imagine Frescati's legal advisers closely reviewing every single word in the chartering agreement the company had reached with Citgo the moment there was any indication at all that the discharge resulted from striking an object while the vessel was docking with Citgo's jetty. A reasonable conclusion at the time would have been that Frescati was in a very strong position to argue that the ultimate responsibility for paying for damages incurred by third parties and for undertaking cleanup was Citgo's alone. Should the Third Circuit's 2018 decision stand (as of this writing, Citgo's appeal is scheduled to be argued before the Supreme Court in November 2019), that is exactly what will happen. Without the oil spill framework provided by OPA, it is very possible that a Cypriot enterprise in the middle of an unfolding disaster of unknown financial implications, in what some claim is the world's most litigious country, would essentially walk away; publicly announce that the far-better positioned Citgo (with 2004 revenues of $32 billion) should clean up the mess, given Citgo's contractual responsibilities; and do little else except respond to lawsuits and cover others' losses when the cases settled years later. Instead, Frescati rolled into action and spent about $100 million in just the first two months, removing oil from the river and its shorelines, vessels, and structures; remediating some of the effects on the local environment; and paying claims for property damage, business disruption, and spill-related expenses.

---

60 The judge overseeing the federal litigation associated with *Deepwater Horizon* indicated that "over 3,000 cases, with well over one hundred thousand claimants/plaintiffs, have been filed." Findings of Fact and Conclusions of Law—Penalty Phase, entered November 30, 2015, at p. 4, in *In re: Oil Spill by the Oil Rig "Deepwater Horizon" in the Gulf of Mexico, on April 20, 2010*, No. 2:10-md-02179 (U.S. District Court, E.D. La.).

To be clear, there are considerable incentives for an RP to take the lead and make an aggressive effort to rapidly deal with the consequences of an oil spill. Managing the cleanup, overseeing the contractors hired to remove oil from shoreline property and vessels, and making the initial call as to whether to pay a property-damage or business-loss claim—and, if so, for how much—provides great control over expenditures. That control would not be available if Frescati had stood down and let the Coast Guard conduct the effort right from the start, using the trust fund as the source for financing the operation. A similar result would have taken place had the Coast Guard decided that Frescati was performing poorly. Indeed, the head of Frescati's oil spill response testified that "if we fail[ed] in any component . . . if we fail[ed] to support our contractors and the contractors fail[ed] to perform in the field with fear of not being paid, for example, the Coast Guard ha[d] full authority to step in and federalize that component of the spill."[61] If that happened, "costs are going to rise dramatically." A potentially more serious outcome could have resulted if Frescati had been perceived as not cooperating in the response. Reportedly, the company continued to pay claims and contractors long after it had reached its limits of liability because of a provision in OPA that can wipe out the cap if the RP has failed "to provide all reasonable cooperation and assistance requested by a responsible official in connection with removal activities."[62] Regardless of Frescati's motivations, the result was a relatively smooth response to a major incident.

Summary

Table 2.1 summarizes key aspects and consequences of the four incidents examined. In all four cases, PRPs provided early assistance as we have defined it for the purposes of this paper, although in the Arkema

---

[61] Memorandum and/or Opinion, entered July 25, 2016, at p. 87, in *United States v. Citgo Asphalt Refining Company*, Case No. 08-cv-2898 and *In re Petition of Frescati Shipping Company, Ltd.*, No. 05-cv-305 (U.S. District Court, E.D. Pa.).

[62] De La Rue and Anderson, 2009, p. 67; 33 U.S.C. § 2703(c)(2).

Table 2.1
Key Features of Four Early Assistance Examples

Incident (State, Year)	Types of Impacts, Damages, and Injuries	Types of Early Assistance	Litigation by Injured Parties	Government Litigation and Sanctions	Possible Impact of Early Assistance on Litigation and Sanctions
CSX tank-car derailment involving acrylonitrile (Tennessee, 2015)	5,000 evacuated; 200 treated for injuries; 46 admitted to hospital; 1 death claimed	Lodging vouchers, food and water, evacuation expenses, remediation of soil contamination	5 putative class actions alleging various losses, including property damage, environmental damage, and personal injury; 10 cases for personal injury and wrongful death	None uncovered	Judge ruled early assistance reduced pool of individuals with potential claims, which contributed to denial of class certification in one case
PG&E natural gas pipeline explosion (California, 2010)	8 killed; 58 injured; 38 homes destroyed; 70 homes damaged; 300 homes evacuated	Costs of losses not covered by insurance; $15K to $50K per household depending on extent of damage; home rebuilding or purchase program; reimbursement of local-government response costs	180 cases involving over 500 plaintiffs ultimately filed, including claims for wrongful death, personal injury, property damage, nuisance, emotional distress; criminal charges filed in federal court	$1.6 billion fine assessed against PRP by California Public Utilities Commission	ALJs acknowledged PG&E's early assistance program in setting a penalty; however, there is no clear evidence that the early assistance efforts carried any weight in the calculation of award size

Table 2.1—Continued

Incident (State, Year)	Types of Impacts, Damages, and Injuries	Types of Early Assistance	Litigation by Injured Parties	Government Litigation and Sanctions	Possible Impact of Early Assistance on Litigation and Sanctions
Arkema organic peroxide combustion (Texas, 2017)	205 residents evacuated	Hotel vouchers; rental cars; gift cards for food, clothing, medicine, and pet care; debris and ash removal	Civil suits by named residents and first responders for personal injuries, loss of earning capacity, mental anguish, real and personal property damaged, etc.; putative class action on behalf of residents and first responders	Civil action for violating various government. codes; a criminal case against Arkema management	None detected
Athos I oil spill (New Jersey, 2004)	Temporarily shut down Port of Philadelphia; affected onshore facilities; killed an estimated 12,000 birds; fouled vessels, structures, and equipment along shore	Over 650 public and private damage claims, including claims for loss in business; PRP paid out $180 million in total cleanup costs, claims, and ship damages	Putative class action for property damage, economic loss, inconvenience, and diminished real estate value; the case was dismissed	United States filed suit seeking reimbursement of payments from OSLTF	Payments through the OPA process resulted in surprisingly few lawsuits.

incident, the assistance efforts became a source of dissatisfaction and community frustration. Also, the assistance provided in the *Athos I* oil spill was shaped by a particular statutory framework that applies to the release of petroleum products in navigable waters of the United States and thus is different in nature than the types of early assistance in the other three examples. Litigation was prevalent in the CSX, PG&E, and Arkema incidents (releases of liability were not required to receive early assistance in these three incidents), and class actions were filed in both the CSX and Arkema incidents. In contrast, there was surprisingly little litigation in the *Athos I* oil spill example, given its profound impact on the surrounding region. It is difficult to determine the extent to which early assistance affected litigation and regulatory outcomes. It appears that early assistance contributed to the denial of the certification of a class action in the CSX claim by reducing the number of injured parties with outstanding uncompensated claims. It may well be that PG&E's aggressive early assistance program reduced fines levied by the CPUC compared with what those fines would have been otherwise, but it is difficult to be sure. The early assistance program in the Arkema case appears to have had little impact on public and private litigation (as well as on criminal prosecution activity), but that may be partly because its early assistance program was not well received. Finally, in the case of the *Athos I* oil spill, the OPA framework appears to have been effective in limiting private litigation at least; but as evident from the *Deepwater Horizon* spill, such success is not guaranteed.

CHAPTER THREE

Stakeholder Views of the Benefits and Drawbacks of Early Assistance

Why is early assistance offered at all by a company that may well find itself on the receiving end of a phalanx of lawsuits? How is early assistance perceived by those who are in need of help following a disaster? We attempted to obtain insight into the answers for these questions primarily through three avenues: a series of telephonic and in-person interviews with knowledgeable actors with experience in situations where early assistance has occurred;[1] two simulation exercises with a diverse set of plaintiffs and defense counsel, academics, and corporate management as participants; and a review of media articles reporting on private and public responses to adverse incidents wherein individuals or companies may bear some legal responsibility for cause or severity.

The discussion below summarizes what we learned from all three sources about the potential benefits and drawbacks of early assistance, which we then organized into the following stakeholder categories:

- Potentially responsible parties (PRPs)
- Insurers
- Victims
- Plaintiff attorneys.

---

[1] We used a nonrandom purposive sampling technique for identifying the 14 participants for our interviews. The sessions took place over a two-year period, ending in 2017. Plaintiffs' attorneys, academics, corporate counsel, insurers, special masters, and defense counsel were included in the interview pool.

Potentially Responsible Parties

Benefits

One comment commonly voiced by a number of outside counsel, members of in-house legal departments, and corporate leaders we contacted was that if a company is reasonably certain it was responsible for causing widespread harm, offering to help in some way at an early point after the onset is simply "the right thing to do." The reasons why doing so was considered "right" depended on the speaker's perspective. One such justification involved improving public relations in the aftermath of adverse publicity, because early assistance was thought to be potentially helpful in fostering a positive image for the PRP as perceived by the affected community (and possibly the future jury pool as well), by consumers of the company's goods and services, and by government agencies that would ultimately be making decisions about the company's future operations and past compliance with regulatory requirements. One interviewee stressed the need to be fully prepared for an adverse event with a robust response plan ready to deploy, otherwise the company would always be "several steps behind" and the early assistance effort would not have the desired results. Having good internal governance, vendors, and contractors ready to go with a phone call (including claims-handling firms) and having lawyers as part of the team were said to be key needs. An interviewee also indicated that preparation was not just for the largest enterprises: "Even mid-sized companies should think about readiness."

Another reason suggested by some interviewees associated with PRPs for offering early assistance would be to reduce the likelihood that potential claimants would move into formal litigation. Early assistance was not believed to have any meaningful effect in minimizing claims advanced by those with personal injuries, substantial property damage, or significant business disruption. Instead, those in the community with relatively minor losses could be removed from the litigation landscape, possibly resulting in reduced transaction costs for the company.

Finally, early assistance was said to be particularly helpful when the company was an employer in the region affected by the incident. Helping to get a community's life back in order would, in turn, help support the company's own workforce, ensuring its employees a safe and sustainable place to live and potentially increasing their likelihood of returning to work when operations returned to some semblance of normality.

Drawbacks

PRPs offered a number of reasons why early assistance might not be an effective business strategy. One concern was that setting up a program to offer assistance soon after the incident unfolded can be perceived as an implicit acceptance of legal responsibility, making it more difficult later on to advance legitimate theories that others share in the blame or that the incident was unavoidable or unpredictable.

Another note of caution involved third-party liability insurers. There was concern that insurers might balk at reimbursing the company for any or all aspects of early assistance efforts, either because the relief offered was not conditioned on obtaining a release or because the assistance went beyond what was strictly needed to address liability exposure. In a similar vein, it was said that if other parties were subsequently found to have some responsibility for the event, they could claim that only payments made for the purpose of addressing tort liabilities would be reimbursable.

Some argued that the effect of early assistance in addressing a company's overall liabilities would be minimal, given that it would be primarily targeted toward relatively low-value losses, such as a few nights in a motel or broken windows. Though the number of individuals and businesses incurring such losses might be high, it would be unlikely for these parties to initiate legal action against the company on an individual-plaintiff basis, regardless of whether assistance was offered. In this view, contingent-fee attorneys would generally decline to take such cases, due to the low stakes, and it would make little financial sense for the victim to pursue litigation by paying counsel an hourly fee. It was asserted that the bulk of a company's exposure would come from the smaller number of high-value losses (such as those associated with the destruction of a home or personal injuries), where payments would be made only in exchange for a full release as with any litigation-related claim settlement.

Even if early assistance could reduce a victim's propensity to sue, some felt that class action litigation could make any such reduction meaningless, given that there would be no bar against defining a proposed class to include victims who have already received aid without signing releases. While, in theory, parties negotiating a settlement could take into account the degree to which class members had been paid previously for their losses, it was claimed that settlement value was generally insensitive to early assistance efforts. Thus, early assistance may cause no reduction in what is subsequently paid by the company to satisfy a class settlement. One interviewee noted that, in his experience, the best approach would be to obtain releases for any aid provided, because anything that allows future liability exposure would be exploited by the plaintiffs' bar. In contrast, another interviewee stated that there was really no way to block later challenges to the validity of a release, given the recipient's need for help, so worrying too much about the scope of the release was probably a wasted effort.

There were also concerns that early assistance efforts might be misinterpreted in ways that would reflect poorly on the PRP. Cash payments could be seen as woefully inadequate responses to a major disaster or as crass attempts to buy off people who are in desperate need of help. Rollouts of assistance programs can also generate negative publicity if problems relating to distribution arise, especially if demand for offered goods, services, or funds exceeds PRP expectations and some victims are turned away, even if only temporarily. One commenter noted that even the American Red Cross has been the target of considerable criticism for some of its relief efforts, even though the organization would have played absolutely no role in causing the disaster and even though its response was voluntary rather than required by law.

Finally, we heard complaints about the lack of any discernable or predictable link between the provision of early assistance and the imposition of post-event sanctions. The argument was that rapid, generous efforts to address the unfortunate consequences of an accident should be viewed as evidence of a sincere desire to acknowledge that the event was the fault of the company and to shoulder the burden of making a community whole. Instead, it was asserted, such actions play little or no role in the assessment of punitive damage awards, the judge's determinations regarding criminal sentencing, or the calculations of civil penalties imposed by regulators.

Insurers

Our discussions with representatives of liability insurers were illuminating, but the presumed diversity of practices within the industry may mean that what we heard reflected relatively unique viewpoints.

Benefits

Our interviewees and simulation participants indicated that, far from being considered potentially problematic behavior on the part of insureds, provision of early assistance was encouraged by insurers to some degree. One insurer described a special fund set aside for certain policies that an insured can easily access for covering victims' evacuation expenses, lodging, minor property damage, minor medical care, remediation, and other immediate costs. This insurer's experienced crisis-management teams provided guidance to the insured in what might be unfamiliar territory (i.e., paying out money to address a bad situation) for a relatively new company. Effort was often spent explaining to the insured that denial doesn't play out well in the long run, especially compared with a "*mea culpa*" strategy, where the company announces that it will take care of the mess it made. Making sure the interests of the insured and the insurer were aligned in regard to early assistance was said by some to be of paramount importance when there were threats of major liability losses. So one important task was to coordinate aid efforts and make sure the insured knew what would be covered and what might be outside the scope of the policy. Insurers also suggested that a key goal was reducing transaction costs as much as possible, in part because such expenses could be unpredictable even when there was good information about the value of losses actually incurred by the affected community. Early assistance efforts that removed low-value claims from consideration were said to help minimize the insured's expenditures for defense counsel in the long run (which would typically be paid by the insurer).

Drawbacks

No drawbacks were identified.

Victims

Benefits

While we did not speak directly with disaster victims, media accounts provide an idea of how early assistance might be perceived by those incurring losses. At least in some instances, relief and remediation assistance by PRPs can fill important gaps in the types of aid available from various sources. In the Arkema incident, relief organizations and government agencies were stretched thin responding to the impact of Harvey across a good portion of Texas, and though, in retrospect, some in the community might have found the company's efforts wanting, there were no other sources to cover the cost of alternative housing in the wake of the evacuation order. In a similar vein, PG&E's programs to help rebuild and repair homes accelerated the physical recovery of the neighborhood and presumably offset some of the financial worry of those with low-limit or high-deductible homeowners policies. To be sure, claims advanced through civil litigation would have eventually reached a similar result, though probably not until the final settlement push on the third anniversary of the explosion and fire. Even when disaster-aid providers are on the scene and actively responding, their efforts can be primarily focused on the most basic needs, such as food and a safe place to sleep. It is difficult to imagine the Red Cross handing out vouchers for rental cars as did PG&E, which allowed evacuees to stay with relatives and friends, shop for necessary supplies, and drive to work the next day.

Another "victim-friendly" aspect of early assistance is that, in many instances, aid appears to have been distributed with a minimum of paperwork. Media accounts suggest that, often, assistance is provided freely with few forms or documentation of losses required. This was not always the case, and we did review complaints about having to produce receipts for lost personal property after the house where such property had been located was reduced to ashes; but typically, there were only minor requirements for receiving immediate aid such as hotel vouchers. That said, provision of more generous assistance, such as that offered through PG&E's housing replacement\repair programs, would have necessitated victims to make a nontrivial investment of time and effort to complete applications and obtain appraisals.

Drawbacks

Despite the potential for addressing needs in the days or months following a disaster with a minimum of fuss, early assistance is unlikely to neutralize all feelings of ill will toward what often appears to be the most obvious cause of the trouble. In the previous chapter's example incidents, only the CSX response appears to have reached essentially all affected within a relatively short span of time (reportedly $500 was promptly paid out to every household impacted by the derailment and fire) and, perhaps as a result, less than 8 percent of the reported 5,000 evacuees were named as plaintiffs in subsequent litigation. In many such instances, however, only a portion of those impacted will actually take the necessary steps (e.g., waiting in line at an assistance center) to avail themselves of a company's aid, with far more victims obtaining help from other sources or simply dealing with issues on their own. For those who did not receive direct aid from the PRP, lasting anger and outrage might be understandable. Add what might be characterized in media reports, press releases, and court pleadings as reckless behavior by the PRP, and it becomes unsurprising that early assistance is sometimes not enough to fix a company's compromised public image.

Plaintiffs' Attorneys

Benefits

Some members of the plaintiffs' bar we spoke to echoed what we heard from those representing corporate interests, in that they also believed that early assistance would be "the right thing to do." For the most part, they thought that a company that was at least partially responsible for a disaster had a clear moral obligation to do whatever possible to reduce the suffering and disruption caused by its actions, and as a responsible corporate citizen, it should not need to be forced to do so by a court judgment or regulator's order.

Drawbacks

Plaintiffs' attorneys voiced concerns that such assistance is sometimes offered primarily to serve a corporation's own interests. In these situations, it was suggested, public announcements of a company's supposed generosity are made only for the purpose of turning the attention of regulators and the affected community away from acts of corporate negligence. Some plaintiffs' attorneys asserted that early assistance has the potential to be employed as a tactic for undercutting victims' efforts to seek punitive damage awards, enabling the company to spend its way out of trouble, and ultimately negating any deterrence of future misbehavior.

Another area of concern was the process itself. The PRP is essentially in sole control of how much is being paid out or given away, without any checks or balances or opportunities to seek review by a third party. In addition, corporate interests were said to be in control in regard to how assistance is described to victims and the public at large, possibly resulting in vulnerable recipients being led to believe that whatever is doled out constitutes all of the relief they are eligible to receive and that seeking the advice of counsel would only result in unnecessary delay and expense.

The issue of releases was repeatedly raised. Victims were said to not always fully understand the implications of signing a formal release of claims, especially in the chaotic days and weeks after their lives have been turned upside down. Consultation with counsel would be vital to protecting victims' interests when releases are in play, but the pressing need to secure a place to live, a means of transportation, or basic living expenses may reduce opportunities to seek professional legal review. One plaintiffs' attorney believed that the most egregious examples of PRPs pressuring victims to waive legal rights to obtain help may be in the past, given greater post-disaster scrutiny by the media and the plaintiffs' bar, but that more subtle forms still exist.

It was asserted that even when assistance is offered without requiring any overt waiver of legal rights, acceptance of such help can effectively undercut a victim's ability to seek full compensation in the future. Generally, a defendant in a tort action that has been found to be liable for losses as the result of a trial verdict can get the award amount reduced by the value of any prior payments it made to the plaintiff (the specific procedures used for reducing the award vary from state to state).[2] Assume, for example, that a disaster victim incurred $20,000 in property damage and that a PRP provided immediate help by paying a contractor for $15,000 worth of repairs without demanding that the victim sign any release. The victim could still sue for $20,000 and receive an award in that amount from a jury, but the judge would likely reduce the verdict to $5,000 in light of the earlier payment (such reduction is commonly referred to as a "setoff"). In theory, the victim would ultimately be made whole once he or she received the remaining $5,000 as satisfaction of the amended judgment. Though an attorney working on a contingency basis might view a $20,000 claim as large enough to yield a fee that justifies the risk of no recovery at trial or by settlement, knowing there had already been substantial payments to the victim and that a setoff would be certain even with a successful trial could result in a decision to decline to take on the case, given that it would result in a recovery of no more than $5,000. Unless a victim hired the attorney for an hourly fee to pursue the remaining $5,000 (an unlikely scenario), the PRP could wind up paying less than the victim's actual losses.

Summary

The example incidents and reactions of stakeholders make it clear that the implementation of early assistance is not an unquestionably beneficial strategy for PRPs, at least not in terms of always reducing future

---

2 See, for example, Restatement (Second) of Torts § 920A ("A payment made by a tortfeasor or by a person acting for him to a person whom he has injured is credited against his tort liability, as are payments made by another who is, or believes he is, subject to the same tort liability") and 22 Am. Jur. 2d Damages § 399 ("Payments made by the defendant to or for the benefit of the plaintiff reduce the recoverable damages").

litigation or improving public opinion. And concerns were voiced that early assistance relies on the uncertain assumption that corporations will refrain from taking advantage of victims at a vulnerable time in their lives. However, there was an overall sense among those interviewed that PRP-provided early assistance was the "right thing to do" and can have a positive impact on outcomes. This kind of aid does appear to fill some critical gaps in the response-relief-recovery cycle, and it makes sense for a well-funded entity that conceivably bears some fault or moral obligation for the disaster to open its checkbook and start helping, even while its legal advisers are considering strategies for minimizing long-term financial exposure. The potential downsides of PRP-led early assistance can detract from its desirability, and in the next chapter we explore how policymakers might be able to reduce barriers and increase incentives for PRP-provided early assistance, should they decide that doing so is in the public's interest.

CHAPTER FOUR

Potential Ways to Encourage PRPs to Provide Early Assistance

In the previous chapter, we identified several drawbacks of early assistance from the viewpoint of PRPs. Therefore, if policymakers want to encourage PRPs to provide early assistance, they might consider

- explicitly including early assistance as a consideration in sentencing guidelines for criminal conduct
- considering early assistance when determining civil statutory sanctions
- clarifying how post-incident behavior affects punitive damages
- applying OPA-like frameworks to high-risk industries.

Encouraging the Provision of Restitution in Sentencing Guidelines for Criminal Conduct

The U.S. Federal Sentencing Guidelines provide U.S. District Court judges with an assessment tool to help decide sentences for corporations found guilty of criminal conduct.[1] The guidelines reduce the severity of potential sentences when the corporation's actions before and after the incident evidence that an "effective compliance and ethics program"

---

[1] State court systems may employ similar guidance, but we focus here on the federal version because many significant man-caused disasters involve businesses accused of violating federal criminal laws and administrative regulations.

was in place.[2] The term "program" is a bit of a misnomer because the guidance is not necessarily about setting up a formal process; rather, it describes a company's actions to prevent similar conduct or further harm from taking place. One criterion for gauging whether such a program is effective is what the corporation did after it became aware that a problem existed. In that light, Section 8B2.1(b)(7) of the Guidelines indicates that judges should determine whether the organization took action to respond appropriately to what had happened:

> After criminal conduct has been detected, the organization shall take reasonable steps to respond appropriately to the criminal conduct and to prevent further similar criminal conduct, including making any necessary modifications to the organization's compliance and ethics program.

As with many published laws, regulations, and court rules, primary legal authority can include the comments of the drafters to help with interpretation and use. The original version of that guideline had no comments to help explain exactly what sort of response was needed, if any. In 2010, the U.S. Sentencing Commission (the federal judicial agency tasked with promoting transparency and proportionality in sentencing, in part by crafting sentencing policies and practices) proposed that the following comment be added to the Guidelines, to make it clear that a company seeking a downward adjustment in any potential criminal sentence must have taken reasonable steps to address the harm caused to victims:

> First, the organization should respond appropriately to the criminal conduct. <u>In the event the criminal conduct has an identifiable victim or victims</u> the organization should take reasonable steps <u>to provide restitution</u> and otherwise remedy the harm resulting from the criminal conduct. Other appropriate responses may include self-reporting, cooperation with authorities, and other forms of remediation.[3] (emphasis added)

---

2 U.S. Sentencing Commission, 2018, § 8B2.1.

3 75 Fed. Reg. 3534 (January 21, 2010).

The public was then given an opportunity to comment on the proposed amendment. While many favored making the "reasonable steps" requirement more explicit as the commission suggested, others, including the Association of Corporate Counsel, the American Bar Association, and the Practitioners Advisory Group to the Commission, were not. One observer characterized the positions of these organizations as follows: ". . . it would be unreasonable to expect restitution where, for example, civil litigation has not run its course and identifiable victims will not release claims as part of a proposed restitution payment."[4]

In the end, a watered-down version was adopted, in which there was no absolute duty to provide restitution when victims could be identified. In essence, it would be up to the company to determine whether restitution was "appropriate":

> First, the organization should respond appropriately to the criminal conduct. The organization should take reasonable steps, as warranted under the circumstances, to remedy the harm resulting from the criminal conduct. These steps may include, where appropriate, providing restitution to identifiable victims, as well as other forms of remediation. Other reasonable steps to respond appropriately to the criminal conduct may include self-reporting and cooperation with authorities.[5]

Adopting the guidance originally proposed by the commission would have been one way to incentivize early assistance, making it clear to a company that found itself as a potential point of origin for a widespread disaster that an aggressive aid program might hedge against receiving the maximum possible criminal sentence. It would be equally helpful to strongly advise judges to consider such actions as persuasive evidence of a desire to address past wrongs.

---

4 Gibson Dunn, 2010.

5 U.S. Sentencing Commission, 2018, § 8B2.1, *Commentary*, effective November 1, 2010.

Considering Early Assistance When Calculating Civil Statutory Sanctions

Another possibility would be to provide similar guidance for judges and regulators when considering the imposition of civil statutory sanctions. EPA enforcement actions for violations of the Clean Air Act,[6] Superfund,[7] Clean Water Act (CWA),[8] or Safe Drinking Water Act,[9] for example, can result in noncriminal fines and penalties of substantial size, sometimes involving tens of millions of dollars (we again focus on federal laws, though a similar approach could be employed in state-level equivalents). The statutory provisions of the CWA provide a useful example of the factors that judges are required to take into account when determining the size of civil penalties:

> In determining the amount of a civil penalty, the court shall consider the seriousness of the violation or violations, the economic benefit (if any) resulting from the violation, any history of such violations, any good-faith efforts to comply with the applicable requirements, the economic impact of the penalty on the violator, and such other matters as justice may require.[10]

To provide guidance to its litigation teams when negotiating settlements with regulated entities believed to be in violation of federal environmental statutes, the EPA has issued various civil-penalty policy statements describing how the penalties should be calculated. While the nature of the formula to be employed for those calculations and the rules for interpreting the formula are statute-specific (the precise guid-

---

6 Clean Air Act Amendments of 1970, Pub. L. 91-604, 84 Stat. 1676 (1970).

7 Comprehensive Environmental Response, Compensation, and Liability Act of 1980, Pub. L. 96-510, 94 Stat 2767 (1980).

8 The term *Clean Water Act* typically refers to the Federal Water Pollution Control Act Amendments of 1972 (Pub. L. 92-500, 86 Stat. 816), as amended by the Clean Water Act of 1977 (Pub. L. 95-217, 91 Stat 1566), as well as other modifications to the 1972 act.

9 The Safe Drinking Water Act (Pub. L. No. 93-523, 88 Stat 1660, 1974) as well as amendments in 1986, 1996, and 2016.

10 33 U.S.C. § 1319(d).

ance for the Clean Air Act differs somewhat from that for Superfund, for example), generally the policy considers whether the party has or will perform environmental mitigation not required by law and the party's ability to pay a potential penalty. It also considers the strength of the EPA's case and, most critically, the "economic benefit" to the party of its noncompliance with EPA mandates and the "gravity" (i.e., seriousness) of the violations.[11]

To promote recovery and remediation in the aftermath of an event, it might be helpful to revise current civil-penalty policy to take into account the effort made by a PRP to provide voluntary assistance (such as offering to cover disruptions in commercial interests, such as fishing boats and agricultural operations) and to engage in aggressive cleanup operations and extensive testing of soil, water, and air. One way to make this happen would be to add an additional consideration to the penalty-calculating policy regarding the degree to which early assistance helped to return a community back to some semblance of normality. A good-faith, appropriately sized effort in this regard could be the basis of a downward adjustment in the potential penalty, similar to what now can result when a regulated entity voluntarily agrees to undertake supplemental environmental projects.

Another way to encourage early assistance might be to include early assistance as a type of offset to the economic-benefit component of the penalty. EPA guidance for certain CWA violations states that the economic-benefit component is intended to place "violators in the same financial position as they would have been if they had complied on time" with applicable regulations.[12] The value of early assistance (such as the dollars spent by a PRP for contractors to visit affected homes and remove toxic substances on the properties) could be subtracted from the economic-benefit subtotal.

---

[11] See, for example, U.S. Environmental Protection Agency, 1995.

[12] U.S. Environmental Protection Agency, 1995, p. 4. The financial savings a company is determined to have realized by forgoing more frequent inspections of equipment as required by agency mandates, for example, would be part of an economic benefit assessment in the aftermath of an incident where such equipment failed and pollutants were released into a water supply as a result.

In a similar vein, early assistance could be factored into the gravity component. The EPA's assessment of the gravity of CWA violations is essentially intended both as a punitive measure and as a deterrence against similar bad behavior by ensuring that the regulated entity is actually worse off than it would have been had it simply obeyed the law in the first place. Gravity is measured by determining a monthly-penalty value for each violation of the law and multiplying that value by the number of months each violation continued. The impact on human health from the discharge of pollutants, for example, would be one consideration in determining the monthly-penalty value. But current EPA guidance also provides for certain "gravity-adjustment factors" that can enhance or reduce overall gravity calculations. One such factor is for a "Quick Settlement Adjustment." EPA's civil penalty policy states that in "order to provide an extra incentive for violators to negotiate quickly and reasonably, and in recognition of a violator's cooperativeness," the agency can reduce the overall gravity amount by 10 percent if it "expects the violator to settle quickly."[13] A similar gravity-adjustment factor, which instead considers whether the violator initiated a good-faith, early assistance program, would presumably incentivize a party's interest in rapidly addressing the consequences of its actions.

Clarifying How Post-Incident Behavior Affects Punitive Damages

Early assistance might be encouraged if PRPs knew that quickly taking appropriate action to help disaster victims could reduce their financial exposure should litigation ensue and a trial results in an award of punitive damages. But Federal Rule of Evidence 407 (FRE 407) generally prohibits the admission of evidence of subsequent measures taken to remediate earlier harms.

---

[13] U.S. Environmental Protection Agency, 1995, p. 13.

> When measures are taken that would have made an earlier injury or harm less likely to occur, evidence of the subsequent measures is not admissible to prove:
> - negligence;
> - culpable conduct;
> - a defect in a product or its design; or
> - a need for a warning or instruction.
>
> But the court may admit this evidence for another purpose, such as impeachment or—if disputed—proving ownership, control, or the feasibility of precautionary measures.[14]

A review of case law and secondary legal authority suggest that FRE 407 is primarily discussed in the context of protecting defendants from unintended negative consequences arising from its positive behavior after an adverse incident. The fact that a company redesigned its product to keep it from exploding, for example, cannot be offered as evidence that the product was, in fact, defective when the plaintiff was injured. Without such a rule, supporters argue, PRPs might be disincentivized from taking corrective action to reduce the likelihood of future harm, since doing so could be used to show that there was something seriously wrong with their products or behavior in the first place. Most state court systems have rules about evidence of subsequent measures that either mirror FRE 407's language or are very similar.

FRE 407 includes an exception that allows evidence to be admitted when it is offered for a purpose other than proving negligence, culpable conduct, defects, or warning necessity. The list of acceptable examples in the rule (such as for proving disputed ownership) is not exhaustive, so courts have essentially unlimited discretion to allow admission as long as proof of negligence, etc., is not intended.[15]

Though the exception is typically used by a plaintiff to submit evidence of a defendant's post-event actions, it can be used by a defendant as well. One way to incentivize PRPs to undertake an early assis-

---

[14] FRE 407.

[15] It should be noted that even if the purpose of offering evidence of subsequent measures does not violate FRE 407, such evidence can still be barred by FRE 403 when the dangers of prejudice or confusion substantially outweigh the evidence's probative value.

tance program would be to make it clear that "another purpose" also includes a defendant attempting to show, in the punitive damage phase of a trial, that it made an appropriate, good-faith effort to address the harms caused by its actions. The purpose of submitting evidence of its restitution or remediation would not be to counter the plaintiff's claims that the defendant behaved in a reckless or outrageous manner (a typical requirement for justifying a punitive damage verdict) but to present an additional factor for the trier of fact to consider when calculating the size of the award, after the underlying liability has already been determined.

Guidance to juries and judges when determining the size of a punitive damage verdict can sometimes be quite thin. Colorado's pattern jury instructions, for example, simply tells jurors that punitive damages "are to punish the defendant and to serve as an example to others."[16] Even when jury instructions provide more concrete guidance for award calculations, they are generally silent as to whether efforts to remediate victim losses are proper aspects for consideration. Case law is not of much help, as few appellate opinions have specifically examined whether evidence of a defendant's post-event conduct can be used to mitigate the size of a punitive damage award.[17] That said, examination of those few opinions suggests that the balance is tipped against such a notion, often on the grounds that "allowing such evidence to be admitted during a punitive damages stage may merely present the bad actor with the opportunity to mitigate punitive damages through use of a recently initiated subsequent remedial measure as window-dressing."[18]

Tennessee law provides a model that might be used as a starting point for creating an express statutory requirement to consider the post-event behavior of defendants in the context of punitive damages, particularly because it speaks to what the defendant might have done to address victim losses:

---

[16] Colo. Jury Instr., Civil 5:4.

[17] "A review of case law from other jurisdictions and academic commentary on this subject reveals no consistent rule on the admissibility of such evidence." *Swinton v. Potomac Corp.*, 270 F.3d 794, 813 (9th Cir. 2001).

[18] Hacker, 1993, p. 995.

> In all cases involving an award of punitive damages, the trier of fact, in determining the amount of punitive damages, shall consider, to the extent relevant . . . whether, once the misconduct became known to defendant, defendant took remedial action or attempted to make amends by offering a prompt and fair settlement for actual harm caused. . . . [19]

In a similar vein, the National Conference of Commissioners on Uniform State Laws' Model Punitive Damages Act also mentions remediation (and the lack thereof) as a factor to be taken into account when assessing the size of an award:

> If a defendant is found liable for punitive damages, a fair and reasonable amount of damages may be awarded. . . . The court shall instruct the jury in determining what constitutes a fair and reasonable amount of punitive damages to consider any evidence that has been admitted regarding the following factors: . . . any remedial measures taken or not taken by the defendant since the wrongful conduct. . . . [20]

Oregon's approach allows the judge to reduce the size of a punitive award if it is shown that reasonable remedial measures have been taken. In this context, however, the specific focus of the term "remedial measures" is on preventing future harm rather than on remedying past harm, as might be accomplished through early assistance:

> [U]pon the motion of a defendant the court may reduce the amount of any judgment requiring the payment of punitive damages entered against the defendant if the defendant establishes that the defendant has taken remedial measures that are reasonable under the circumstances to prevent reoccurrence of the conduct that gave rise to the claim for punitive damages.[21]

---

[19] Tenn. Code Ann. § 29-39-104(a)(4).

[20] National Conference of Commissioners on Uniform State Laws, 1996, p. 18.

[21] Or. Rev. Stat. § 31.730(3).

Texas is another jurisdiction where evidence of remediation might be allowed but not necessarily considered as evidence of efforts to help prior victims. The "situation and sensibilities of the parties" is one factor reviewing courts are to consider when determining whether a punitive damage award is excessive, and the phrase "refers to evidence of such things as remorse, remedial measures, and ability to pay the punitive damages" (emphasis added).[22] But while Texas courts allow the submission of evidence of a defendant's "settlement amounts for punitive damages or prior punitive damages awards that the defendant has actually paid for the same course of conduct," the "actual damage amounts paid by settlements or by judgments" would be considered evidence "that is not relevant, or is unduly prejudicial, and thus, not admissible to mitigate punitive damages."[23] In other words, a defendant can raise the issue of prior punitive damage payments when trying to reduce a potential punitive judgment, but it cannot tell the jury about prior payments for losses that would be considered a form of compensatory or actual damages. To the extent that early assistance efforts, such as rapid payments for property damage and the like, are considered to be settlement regardless of whether a release was involved, they would be inadmissible under current policy.

Perhaps the most notable instance of early assistance being considered as part of the assessment of punitive damage award size occurred in the litigation surrounding the *Exxon Valdez* oil spill. The original jury verdict against the oil company in a 1994 federal trial (five years after the spill) awarded the plaintiffs $287 million in compensatory damages and $5 billion in punitive damages. In 2001 the federal Court of Appeals for the Ninth Circuit sent the case back to the district court judge for reconsideration. One reason given the appellate court gave for overruling the original verdict was that the punitive award was excessive, in part because the ratio of punitive damages to compensatory damages was over 17 to 1, far larger than a 4-to-1 ratio in a case the U.S. Supreme Court had recently asserted to be "close to the

[22] *Ellis Cty. State Bank v. Keever*, 936 S.W.2d 683, 688 (Tex. App. 1996).

[23] *Owens-Corning Fiberglas Corp. v. Malone*, 972 S.W.2d 35, 41 (Tex. 1998).

line" beyond which a punitive award could be considered disproportional to the underlying harm. As part of its decision, the Ninth Circuit opined that the proper way to calculate such a ratio would be to use an adjusted value for the compensatory award that is exclusive of the expenses the defendant incurred to address the consequences of its actions: "The amount that a defendant voluntarily pays before judgment should generally not be used as part of the numerator, because that would deter settlements prior to judgment."[24] The court seemed to suggest that many of Exxon's earlier expenditures such as "settlements with private parties," "settlements with government entities," and "the costs of clean up" could be excluded from the value of the compensatory award for the purpose of calculating the ratio. Such an exclusion would presumably result in a much higher ratio than 17 to 1 and as such in a punitive award even more disproportional to the related compensatory award than what the U.S. Supreme Court might have considered reasonable at the time.

When the case was remanded to the federal district court for reconsideration and a revised ruling on the verdict was eventually issued in 2002 by the trial judge, his decision was sharply critical of what he "found to be the most troubling aspect of the decision of the court of appeals in *In re Exxon Valdez*."[25] He felt that the appellate court's conclusion that voluntary payments prior to judgment should be excluded from the calculation of the punitive-to-compensatory ratio was without "citation of authority, and without explanation that has a nexus to the due process-fair notice issue which underlies the question of whether or not punitive damages are grossly excessive." Bluntly stating that the "briefing of the parties and the court's independent research suggest that authority in support of the foregoing proposition is nonexistent, and what sparse authority does exist reaches a contrary

[24] *In re Exxon Valdez*, 270 F.3d 1215, 1244 (9th Cir. 2001). The appellate court's use of the word *numerator* appears to stem from overly casual use of the term, as the reference was to the right side of the 17:1 ratio that represents the compensatory award component (the relevant fraction here would be $5 billion/$287 million, and so, technically, the compensatory award would be the *denominator*).

[25] *In re Exxon Valdez*, 236 F.Supp.2d 1043, 1060 (D. Alaska 2002).

conclusion," he apparently considered the argument that not accounting for prior voluntary payments when determining punitive award size would deter settlements to be without foundation:

> This court does not understand how or why encouraging settlements should be a part of the due process analysis of a punitive damages award made in a case which went to trial. Moreover, this court believes that a contrary argument is more logical. If a defendant knows that it will get credit for a partial settlement, voluntarily made before trial, it may be encouraged to go to trial; whereas, as a general proposition the specter of a large punitive damages award is a very powerful factor in encouraging settlements of entire cases. Reducing the risk of going to trial on punitive damages by discounting them for voluntary payments does not encourage settlements, it encourages trials.[26]

In addition to ignoring the appellate court's order to factor into the calculation of the punitive award all voluntary expenditures Exxon had made for early assistance and other purposes, the judge suggested that reducing

> . . . actual harm for purposes of ratio analysis by the amount of voluntary payments unfairly skews the ratio in Exxon's favor, and in effect gives Exxon double credit for voluntary payments by reducing both punitive damages and actual harm for purposes of the punitive damages/harm ratio analysis.[27]

It should be noted that the trial judge did reduce the punitive damage award at this time to $4 billion in order to comply with the Ninth Circuit's original order to adjust its size downward, but the basis for doing so was not related to the basis of the ratio calculation or any aspect involving early assistance.

That ruling did not put an end to the matter. After yet another landmark U.S. Supreme Court ruling on punitive damages and how

---

[26] *In re Exxon Valdez*, 236 F.Supp.2d at 1060–1061 (D. Alaska 2002).

[27] *In re Exxon Valdez*, 236 F.Supp.2d at 1061 (D. Alaska 2002).

they should be reviewed when claimed to be excessive,[28] the Ninth Circuit simply vacated the trial judge's 2002 order and once again remanded the matter back to the district court for reconsideration. The revised ruling was issued by the district court in 2004 and, this time, the trial judge restated his opposition to the notion that post-event expenditures should be factored into the calculation of punitive award size (to be precise, he essentially repeated his discussion from the earlier ruling); but he went further, deciding that the original verdict of $5 billion was, in fact, constitutionally permissible, reducing it by just $500,000 to again comply with the downward-adjustment order.

As might be expected, the Ninth Circuit saw the issue in a very different light when the matter again went on appeal. In 2006 it restated its belief that, in general, voluntary payments made by a defendant in the aftermath of an adverse incident should be taken out of the calculations of how the punitive award compares to the compensatory award. It also indicated that the millions of dollars Exxon spent in compensation after the spill mitigated both the harm incurred by those who received such payments and the level of reprehensibility of the company's conduct. But it seemed to back off in the application of those assumptions, in part, by focusing on its earlier phrasing that the "amount that a defendant voluntarily pays before judgment should generally not be used as part of the numerator" (emphasis added). To put it succinctly, the Court of Appeals now felt that the *Exxon Valdez* situation was not a good fit for the general rule.

By this point in the ongoing litigation, the size of the calculated harm from the spill had risen from the $285 million determined by the jury's original verdict to $513 million, based on subsequent judgments and recoveries. The Court of Appeals was not fully receptive to Exxon's argument that, given the $493 million it had paid through the company's voluntary claims programs and other settlements, and given the language in the 2001 Ninth Circuit ruling, the adjusted value of the harm for excessive punitive award consideration would be about $20 million. That value would mean that even a 9-to-1 ratio (the apparent upper

[28] *State Farm Mutual Automobile Ins. Co. v. Campbell*, 538 U.S. 408 (2003).

limit on punitive awards the U.S. Supreme Court was then willing to agree to outside of cases involving personal injuries and intentional acts) would result in a punitive award of no more than $183 million, about 4 percent of the district court's previous order. Though the appellate court recognized "that Exxon, soon after the spill, instituted a claims payment system that almost fully compensated plaintiffs for their economic losses and did so promptly" and that "Exxon's prompt payment of compensatory damages should be a substantial mitigating factor in our review of punitives," it now felt that an "important subsidiary issue is the extent to which we are bound to give literal effect to the sentences in our earlier opinion concerning subtracting the pre-judgment payments from actual harm. . . ."[29] Apparently it did not feel very bound at all to the literal interpretation. While noting that "we have already held that mitigation is both relevant and conscientious in the toxic-tort setting" and that it "would be unwise in reviewing punitive damages to ignore the prompt steps of a defendant to take curative action in a mass tort case," it also asserted that a "defendant cannot buy full immunity from punitive damages by paying the likely amount of compensatory damages before judgment."[30] Deciding now that only $9 million could be supported as a reasonable deduction from the $513 million total loss for the purpose of calculating punitive award size, the appeals court held that, with the most recent $4.5 billion punitive award, the ratio was now just at 8.93 to 1, "a proportion bordering on the presumption of constitutional questionability."[31]

But even though "Exxon's conduct was particularly egregious and involved significant economic damages," its "conduct was not intentional and it promptly took steps to ameliorate the harm it caused." As a result,

> . . . [m]itigating factors also come into play. Exxon instituted prompt efforts to clean up the spill and to compensate the plain-

---

29 *In re Exxon Valdez*, 472 F.3d, 600, 611 (9th Cir. 2006).

30 *In re Exxon Valdez*, 472 F.3d, 621 (9th Cir. 2006).

31 *In re Exxon Valdez*, 472 F.3d, 623 (9th Cir. 2006).

> tiffs for their economic harm. As we earlier observed, if a defendant acts promptly to ameliorate harm for which it is responsible, the size of a punitive damages award should be reduced to encourage socially beneficial behavior. . . . Moreover, the costs that Exxon incurred in compensating the plaintiffs and cleaning up the oil spill have already substantially served the purposes of deterrence, lessening the need for a high punitive damages award.[32]

In the end, the court concluded that a ratio of more than 5 to 1 would violate controlling due process standards, so it adjusted the punitive award down to exactly a 5-to-1 ratio, yielding $2.5 billion in damages (based on $504 million in harm); and as a final parting shot, it wearily stated that it was "time for this protracted litigation to end."

It did not end, however—at least not then. The matter finally made its way to the U.S. Supreme Court, which, in 2008, issued its opinion on the appeal from the 2006 Ninth Circuit holding. It essentially ignored the back-and-forth between the district court and the court of appeals on the question of Exxon's early assistance and other actions taken in response to the spill. Instead, it simply decided that, based partly on empirical research on observed ratios of punitive damages to compensatory damages in past cases, a 1-to-1 ratio "is a fair upper limit in such maritime cases" and that it took "for granted the District Court's calculation of the total relevant compensatory damages at $507.5 million."[33] At that point the math was quite straightforward, with the punitive award likewise being set at exactly $507.5 million.

As can be seen, the issue of how post-incident behaviors by a PRP can affect the size of a punitive damage award is far from settled. Given that the legal authority for assessing punitive damages is, for the most part, the province of the legislatures and appellate courts of the individual states (*Exxon Valdez* was arguably a unique situation in that it was a relatively rare application of federal common law), moving toward a uniform, national standard, in which evidence of early assistance can be

---

[32] *In re Exxon Valdez*, 472 F.3d, 624 (9th Cir. 2006).

[33] *Exxon Shipping Co. v. Baker*, 554 U.S. 471, 488 (fn. 13), 513, 515 (2008).

used to mitigate punitive damage awards. would probably not be easy. Nevertheless, a state interested in encouraging corporations within its borders to respond quickly and robustly to disasters potentially of their own making might consider reexamining its rules for assessing the size of punitive awards.

Utilizing OPA-Like Frameworks

Our final suggested approach toward incentivizing early assistance involves applying a framework similar to that of OPA to activities conducted in high-risk industries (other than those already within OPA's jurisdiction, such as industries that transport, store, refine, extract, or use petroleum products).

As indicated earlier, OPA appears to offer an efficient approach, dealing with thousands of discharges each year, the vast majority of which are handled in relative quiet, address consequences as a matter of routine, and keep victims from incurring high transaction costs to recover a wide range of damages. Perhaps a similar program could be set up for specific commercial activities for which a rapid response by PRPs is desired.

Establishing complex legal regimes for handling disaster response and claims is not without precedent. Incidents at commercial nuclear power plants within the scope of the Price-Anderson Act, for example, mirror OPA in some ways, in terms of setting limits on liability for plant owners and operators and in spreading risk through industry-wide assessments.[34] In the event of a particular type of incident, known as an extraordinary nuclear occurrence, there would be a somewhat less onerous path to compensation than with traditional litigation.[35]

---

[34] Pub. L. 85-256, 71 Stat. 576, 1957. See also Chapter Six in Pace and Dixon, 2017.

[35] Not every industrial facility has the potential for the catastrophic multistate harm that a nuclear power plant possesses, but many can, under the right circumstances, cause serious disruption of the surrounding community in terms of physical damage, environmental impact, business disruption, and personal injuries. Examples include facilities manufacturing, transporting, or storing certain chemicals or products (e.g., anhydrous and aqueous ammonia, arsenic, butane and isobutane, chlorine, cyanide compounds, dioxins, formal-

Once the industry or activity is selected as the focus of the legal framework, rules would have to be drafted for singling out the most likely cause of a disaster, ideally a source that has the greatest financial interest in the stream of commerce related to the product or material. One possibility would be to mirror OPA's approach in using the physical site of the release as the primary criterion for identifying the source, even if legal responsibility might be more properly associated with another actor. For example, if a private plane accidently crashed into a storage tank and triggered a chemical release, the owner or operator of the storage tank would be the initial recipient of the designation even if pilot error was the proximate cause.

A means for creating revenue to build a trust fund for financing post-event relief and remediation would be needed. One possibility would be to impose excise taxes on the manufacture, production, or importation of the product in question, similar to what is now done for childhood vaccines.[36]

The limit on a designated party's liability would have to be set at a point high enough for it to consider (and ultimately pay for) claims by those within the affected zone in the most likely worst-case disaster. In instances where the PRP cannot or does not desire to handle the claims process, a government agency experienced in such matters would stand in the PRP's shoes (like in OPA), and at some later point the agency would seek to recover associated expenses from the PRP or some other tortfeasor. In instances where the PRP paid claims and performed other remedial activities but believed others were ultimately responsible, it could seek contribution through the civil justice system at its convenience. If the tortfeasors disappeared or were assetless, then that same party could proceed against the liability trust fund.

Policymakers would have to decide on appropriate incentives to encourage the PRP to cooperate with various features of the program.

---

dehyde, hydrochloric acid, nitrogen fertilizers, sulfur dioxide, volatile organics, industrial propane, pesticides, and fireworks), coal mines and associated facilities, levees and dams, sewage plants (often using large amounts of chlorine gas), biohazard facilities, airports, electric power generating plants, and even poultry processors.

[36] See Chapter Seven in Pace and Dixon, 2017.

OPA and the Price-Anderson Act use limitations on liability as the dangling carrot, but given repeated concerns that any liability cap set too low could negatively impact safety culture,[37] the set of incentives would need to be carefully chosen.

Arguably the primary difficulty in setting up such a program would not be its design and implementation, but instead the marshaling of sufficient levels of political will to push the proposed law through the legislature. For passage, OPA required *Exxon Valdez*, while various vaccine programs required potential shortages of critical medicines or the threat of terrorism. Getting across the legislative threshold in a time without a unifying crisis will be a daunting challenge.

The final issue would be to decide whether to set up a national program or multiple ones at the state level. Congressional action may be the most difficult to achieve given the diversity of interested stakeholders across the nation, but separate state programs run the risk of driving affected businesses to neighboring states without such rules.[38] For some high-volume/high-demand/high-risk industries, such as those dealing with anhydrous ammonia, the attraction of a profitable market may offset any initial reaction to take the business elsewhere, but low-volume businesses may not be as fortunate.

---

[37] See Chapter Eight in Pace and Dixon, 2017.

[38] Depending on the how the program was structured (e.g., with low liability limits), a state program could, in principle, encourage businesses to move in from neighboring states.

CHAPTER FIVE

Concluding Thoughts

In terms of dealing with the most challenging consequences of a disaster, early assistance can pale in comparison with the actions of first responders who put their lives on the line; the activities of aid organizations that set up operations days before the onset of a predicted event and work 24 hours a day until the situation has stabilized; and the efforts of members of the affected community who selflessly give up their time, effort, and money to help total strangers move forward in the face of adversity. In many instances, a company itself, regardless of its role in causing the disaster, is adversely impacted, sometimes losing employees to death and serious injury, facing financial ruin, and suffering total destruction of its property and facilities. In such instances, any expectation that the company can meaningfully participate in the long-term recovery of nearby neighborhoods and commercial districts is obviously misplaced. Even when the company emerges from the smoke relatively unscathed, its assets, experiences, and capabilities may be completely overwhelmed by the scope of the disaster it has wrought. Liability insurers play an important role in these situations, standing in the shoes of the essentially paralyzed enterprise and, at least, offering victims potential funding for covering losses incurred through no fault of their own.

But there are many instances where the PRP indeed has the financial resources to step up and provide direct help in the immediate aftermath; just as, importantly, it also has the physical assets and personnel to make that happen. It is always risky to make broad generalizations about any sort of human activity, but in conducting our research for this paper, it was difficult not to come away with a sense that, very often, relatively larger disasters are associated with relatively larger enterprises. Obviously, the correlation does not always hold (it is certainly possible that a one-person landscaping service using a gas mower on dry grass can trigger a massive wildfire), but the big explosions, big spills, and big toxic releases all seemed to involve big companies, or at least ones with operations and corporate offices that extended beyond the specific site of the incident.[1] A possible explanation for this impression is that, often, the severity of the disaster is related to the scope of the underlying commercial activity, such as the storage of a half million pounds of aluminum nitrate, the construction and maintenance of massive natural-gas pipelines, the operations of aircraft capable of transporting over 200 passengers each, the shipment of millions of gallons of crude oil by sea, the interstate railroads running trains with over 100 tank cars, the grain elevators capable of storing millions of bushels, and so on. Only enterprises with significant financial wherewithal have the capability to operate at these levels. Given the nature of such operations and the known risks involved, these companies have the assets and the expertise to prepare well in advance of an emergency and to maintain an ability to quickly deliver aid across its economic footprint. They also have the ability to hire excellent outside counsel, ones that have the legal acumen to protect the company's long-term financial and litigation exposure, even as its employees are handing out vouchers and cash to cover residents' expenses while apologizing profusely and with great sincerity. These types of business enterprises have the capability to implement early assistance programs, and we have attempted to characterize the benefits and downsides of doing so.[2] Our goals,

---

[1] In southern Oregon in 2015, a single lawnmower illegally operating during a restricted time of day triggered a fire that burned 26,452 acres and involved the efforts of over 800 firefighters.

[2] None of the four companies in the example incidents in Chapter Two were either completely unprepared for what happened or reticent about providing early assistance to the affected region. Three had incident response teams from other parts of its organization in place soon after evacuations were ordered, while in Frescati's situation, it hired an experienced spill contractor within hours of discovering the spill. Arkema's efforts to provide early assistance were not as well received as the others, though it is difficult to discern how

however, were limited to describing how early assistance occurred in four admittedly unique instances and how some possible changes in the substantive and procedural law might incentivize PRPs to take a more active role. The paper is not meant to address fundamental issues in disaster-response policy, suggest that PRPs can always be more effective in the post-disaster context than traditional responders (such as the Red Cross or FEMA), or advocate for implementation of any of the potential legal changes.

After weighing the benefits and drawbacks, policymakers may choose to encourage PRPs to play a role in providing early assistance. Tweaking the guidelines for corporate criminal sentencing, adjusting the severity of civil sanctions downward when the company conducts a good-faith early assistance program, and considering a company's mitigation efforts when deciding on the size of a punitive damage award are all ways that might encourage companies to provide early assistance (rather than letting the Red Cross do the heavy lifting and to wait it out in relative silence until all of the lawsuits are fully resolved, maybe five years later). However, decisions on whether to push for such policies should also consider the extent to which any change in the law might provide well-financed companies the luxury of spending their way out of a large fine or punitive damage award, which would undercut any deterrence against future bad behavior. Such decisions should also consider the potential for uncoordinated responses by multiple parties (i.e., PRPs, government, and nonprofits), which could result in duplication of effort and waste.

Policymakers may be concerned that increasing incentives for early assistance could result in unwanted consequences, but there may be ways to mitigate those concerns. One way might be to give the greatest weight to early assistance provided the first day of the incident—when the need is most acute and liability most uncertain—and the

---

much of the community's negative reaction was due to the aid program's own Harvey-caused issues with logistics and communications, how much was due to the assistance being viewed through the public lens of a potentially catastrophic event that was shrouded in much mystery and confusion, and how much was due to a widely held belief that the situation could have been avoided entirely with better preparation for a forecasted weather event.

least weight to aid rolled out after many months, once investigative reports are in and lawyers are deep into the civil pretrial process. Efforts of smaller enterprises could be assessed not by how much money they spend but by the degree to which they cooperate with governmental agencies and participate in the recovery effort over the long haul. No doubt there are other strategies, but, ultimately, the entire spectrum of stakeholders (PRPs, the plaintiffs' bar, liability insurers, regulators, etc.) must collaborate to determine the best ways to retain the traditional deterrence mechanisms of sanctions, fines, and punitive awards, while promoting the idea of early assistance and accelerating the pace at which a community gets back on its feet.

References

Arkema, Inc., *Comments from Rich Rowe, President & CEO, Arkema Inc. on Our Site in Crosby, Texas*, August 30, 2017a. As of September 12, 2018: https://www.arkema-americas.com/en/social-responsibility/incident-page-2/presidents-message/

———, *Arkema Holds Press Conference, Focuses on Community Outreach*, September 4, 2017b. As of September 13, 2018: https://www.arkema-americas.com/export/sites/americas/.content/medias/downloads/social-responsibility/20190904-transcript-press-conference-arkema-inc-crosby.pdf

———, *Arkema Inc. Crosby Update at 1:00pm EDT September 17, 2017*, September 17, 2017c. As of September 14, 2018: https://www.arkema-americas.com/en/social-responsibility/incident-page-2/previous-update-statements/

———, *Arkema Inc. Statement—October 6, 2017—5:00PM EDT*, October 6, 2017d. As of September 14, 2018: https://www.arkema-americas.com/en/social-responsibility/incident-page-2/previous-update-statements/

———, *Arkema Inc. Update—December 11, 2017—3:00PM EST*, December 11, 2017e. As of September 14, 2018: https://www.arkema-americas.com/en/social-responsibility/incident-page-2/previous-update-statements/

Associated Press, "Citgo Cleared of $177M Cleanup of Delaware River in Paulsboro After 2004 Oil Spill," *NJ Advance Media*, April 14, 2011. As of August 29, 2018: https://www.nj.com/news/index.ssf/2011/04/citgo_cleared_of_177m_cleanup.html

Bales-Sherrod, Lesli, "Cities Seek More than $226K from CSX for Emergency Response Expenses," *Daily Times*, August 26, 2015. As of September 12, 2018: https://www.thedailytimes.com/news/cities-seek-more-than-k-from-csx-for-emergency-response/article_8391e96c-3e04-50c2-8a41-da395ead8789.html?mode=jqm

Beecken, Stephanie, "1 Year after Maryville Train Derailment, Lawsuits Keep Moving Forward," *WATE 6*, June 30, 2016. As of July 19, 2018: https://www.wate.com/news/local-news/1-year-after-maryville-train-derailment-lawsuits-keep-moving-forward_20170818075604947/92835761

Blakinger, Keri, "Liberty County Sues Arkema for $1 Million over Harvey Disaster," *Houston Chronicle*, March 12, 2018. As of September 27, 2018: https://www.chron.com/news/houston-texas/article/Liberty-County-sues-Arkema-for-1-million-over-12746382.php

Bowe, Rebecca, and Lisa Pickoff-White, "Five Years After Deadly San Bruno Explosion: Are We Safer?" *KQED News*, September 8, 2015. As of May 4, 2018: https://www.kqed.org/news/10667274/five-years-after-deadly-san-bruno-explosion-are-we-safer

Boyajian, David, "The Athos I," presentation given at the Washington Public Ports Association 2016 annual meeting, October 19, 2016. As of September 3, 2018: https://static1.squarespace.com/static/5a8499e518b27dc83c2403ce/t/5bc0d56353450ae7c17f71ea/1539364202549/CLE-2-ATHOS-I-David-Boyajian-Schwabe.pdf

Brooks, Jon, "Despite $1.6 Billion Fine, CPUC President Questions Ability to Police PG&E," *KQED*, April 9, 2015. As of August 3, 2018: https://www.kqed.org/news/10483976/cpuc-approves-1-6-billion-fine-for-pge-over-san-bruno-disaster

Bulwa, Demian, "PG&E Could Face San Bruno Punitive Damages," *SFGate*, October 30, 2012. As of October 23, 2018: https://www.sfgate.com/bayarea/article/PG-amp-E-could-face-San-Bruno-punitive-damages-3994708.php

California Public Utilities Commission, "CPUC Penalizes PG&E $1.6 Billion for Pipeline Violations," press release, April 9, 2015. As of September 23, 2018: http://docs.cpuc.ca.gov/PublishedDocs/Published/G000/M151/K034/151034091.PDF

CBS SF BayArea, "PG&E Sets Up $100 Million 'Rebuild San Bruno' Fund," September 13, 2010. As of May 30, 2018: https://sanfrancisco.cbslocal.com/2010/09/13/pge-sets-up-100-million-rebuild-san-bruno-fund/

Colorado Rules of Civil Procedure Relating to Jury Instructions, Chapter 5, General Instructions Relating to Damages; Instruction 5:4, Exemplary or Punitive Damages. As of August 20, 2019: https://www.courts.state.co.us/userfiles/file/Court_Probation/Supreme_Court/Committees/Civil_Jury_Instructions_Committee/2018/Chapter%205.pdf

Crowe, Michael, "First Lawsuit Filed Following Maryville Rail Car Derailment," *Reno Gazette Journal*, July 10, 2015. As of August 24, 2018: https://www.rgj.com/story/news/2015/07/10/maryville-lawsuit-filed/29991687/

CSX, *Updated CSX Statement/Outreach Center Established—3:30 p.m. July 2, 2015*, July 2, 2015a. As of September 3, 2018:
https://www.csx.com/index.cfm/about-us/media/press-releases/updated-csx-statementoutreach-center-established-330-pm-july-2-2015/

———, *Updated CSX Statement/Outreach Center Established—7 p.m., July 2, 2015*, July 2, 2015b. As of September 6, 2018:
https://www.csx.com/index.cfm/about-us/media/press-releases/updated-csx-statementoutreach-center-established-7-pm-july-2-2015/

———, *Updated CSX Statement/Outreach Center Established*, July 2, 2015c. As of September 2, 2018:
https://www.csx.com/index.cfm/about-us/media/press-releases/updated-csx-statementoutreach-center-established//

Daily Times, "A Timeline of Events Following the 2015 CSX Derailment," July 2, 2017. As of July 17, 2018:
https://www.thedailytimes.com/news/a-timeline-of-events-following-the-csx-derailment/article_2fb54801-331e-5473-9517-a00de6ccf315.html

Dakss, Brian, "Rush To Clean 'Significant' Spill," *CBS News*, November 27, 2004. As of September 5, 2018:
https://www.cbsnews.com/news/rush-to-clean-significant-spill/

Davidson, Rachel A., James Kendra, Sizheng Li, Laurie C. Long, David A. McEntire, Charles Scawthorn, and Joshua Kelly, *San Bruno California, September 9, 2010 Gas Pipeline Explosion and Fire*, University of Delaware Disaster Research Center, May 2012. As of September 6, 2018:
https://www.academia.edu/4435007/San_Bruno_California_September_9_2010_Gas_Pipeline_Explosion_and_Fire

De La Rue, Colin, and Charles B. Anderson, *Shipping and the Environment, 2nd Edition*, Informa, March 2009.

Dempsey, Matt, and Keri Blakinger, "Harris County Sues Arkema for Chemical Disaster During Harvey," *Houston Chronicle*, November 17, 2017. As of September 23, 2018:
https://www.chron.com/news/houston-texas/article/Harris-County-sues-Arkema-for-chemical-disaster-12363560.php

Dempsey, Matt, Keri Blakinger, and Lindsay Ellis, "2 More Chemical Containers Explode at Crosby Chemical Plant," *Houston Chronicle*, September 2, 2017. As of December 4, 2018:
https://www.houstonchronicle.com/news/houston-texas/article/Second-of-chemicals-erupt-at-flooded-Arkema-plant-12166702.php?t=5976cbdc4a

Dudnick, Laura, and Jonah Owen Lamb, "PG&E Convicted in Criminal Pipeline Safety Trial," *San Francisco Examiner*, August 9, 2016. As of August 28, 2018:
http://www.sfexaminer.com/pge-convicted-six-12-charges-criminal-pipeline-safety-trial/

Federal Railroad Administration, Office of Safety Analysis, webpage, undated. As of November 1, 2019:
https://safetydata.fra.dot.gov/OfficeofSafety/publicsite/query/TrainAccidentDamage.aspx

Federal Rules of Evidence, Article IV, Relevance and Its Limits; Rule 403, Excluding Relevant Evidence for Prejudice, Confusion, Waste of Time, or Other Reasons, 2019. As of August 20, 2019:
https://www.rulesofevidence.org/article-iv/rule-403/

Federal Rules of Evidence, Article IV, Relevance and Its Limits; Rule 407, Subsequent Remedial Measures, 2019. As of August 20, 2019:
https://www.rulesofevidence.org/article-iv/rule-407/

Feuk, Melanie, "Crosby Residents Describe Arkema's Impact on Their Homes and Families," *Houston Chronicle*, September 10, 2017. As of June 7, 2018:
https://www.chron.com/neighborhood/lakehouston/news/article/Crosby-residents-share-Arkema-accounts-12178205.php

Gallagher, John, "Judge Orders USD99.5 Million Compensation over *Athos I* Spill," *Fairplay*, July 27, 2016. As of August 31, 2018:
http://www.shippingherald.com/judge-orders-usd99-5-million-compensation-over-athos-i-spill/

George, Jason, "Delaware River Oil Spill Leaves Wildlife Imperiled," *New York Times*, November 29, 2004. As of September 11, 2018:
https://www.nytimes.com/2004/11/29/nyregion/delaware-river-oil-spill-leaves-wildlife-imperiled.html

Gibson Dunn, *U.S. Sentencing Commission Amends Requirements for an Effective Compliance and Ethics Program*, April 13, 2010. As of October 3, 2018:
https://www.gibsondunn.com/u-s-sentencing-commission-amends-requirements-for-an-effective-compliance-and-ethics-program/

Hacker, P. Steven, "Tennessee Attempts to Tighten the Purse Strings on Punitive Damages: Hodges v. S.C. Toof & Co.," *Tennessee Law Review*, Vol. 60, 1993, pp. 983–1004.

Hajna, Lawrence, "Boat, Marina Owners File Oil-Damage Claims," *Courier-Post*, December 2, 2004. As of November 5, 2018:
https://www.thebassbarn.com/forum/4-home-port/2607-angler-s-oil-spill-stories-along-del-river-2.html

———, "Owners Face Long Wait on Spill Claims," *Courier-Post*, March 4, 2005. As of November 1, 2018:
https://www.marine-marketing.gr/newsclip.php?file=200509.txt

Horton, Alex, Amy B. Wang, and Lindsey Bever, “Explosions Possible After ‘Pops’ Heard at Storm-Crippled Texas Chemical Plant, Officials Say,” *Washington Post*, August 31, 2017. As of July 23, 2018:
https://www.washingtonpost.com/news/post-nation/wp/2017/08/30/texas-town-under-emergency-evacuation-as-flooded-chemical-plant-nears-explosion/?utm_term=.1bbdb36c4681

Jacobs Consultancy, *Report of the Independent Review Panel—San Bruno Explosion—Prepared for California Public Utilities Commission*, June 8, 2011. As of August 15, 2018:
https://www.aga.org/sites/default/files/cpuc_independent_review_panel_report_on_san_bruno_expolosion_0.pdf

KHOU, “Evacuees Wait in Long Lines for Aid from Arkema Reps,” September 2, 2017. As of June 3, 2018:
https://www.khou.com/article/news/local/evacuees-wait-in-long-lines-for-aid-from-arkema-reps/470358389

Kindelan, Katie, “San Bruno Fire Heats Up Twitter,” *Adweek*, September 13, 2010. As of May 23, 2018:
https://www.adweek.com/digital/san-bruno-fire/

Kuzydym, Stephanie, and Scott Noll, “Crosby Residents File Second Lawsuit Against Arkema Following Crosby Plant Explosion,” *KHOU*, October 3, 2017. As of October 4, 2018:
https://www.khou.com/article/news/local/crosby-residents-file-second-lawsuit-against-arkema-following-crosby-plant-explosion/480592060

Megargee, Steve, and Johnny Clark, “Officials Lift Evacuation After Tennessee Train Derailment,” *Seattle Times*, July 3, 2015. As of August 27, 2018:
https://www.seattletimes.com/nation-world/nation/officials-to-begin-lifting-evacuation-after-train-derailment/

Melvin, Joshua, “Waiting to Be Made Whole, One Year After the San Bruno Blast,” *Mercury News*, September 3, 2011. As of July 7, 2018:
https://www.mercurynews.com/2011/09/03/waiting-to-be-made-whole-one-year-after-the-san-bruno-blast/

Meyer, Robinson, “Hurricane Harvey Is the Rainiest Atlantic Hurricane Ever Measured,” *The Atlantic*, August 29, 2017. As of August 12, 2018:
https://www.theatlantic.com/science/archive/2017/08/hurricane-harvey-is-the-rainiest-atlantic-hurricane-ever-measured/538407/

Mondlock, Jeff, “Lawyers Meet with Potential Train Derailment Victims,” *WBIR*, July 22, 2015. As of October 23, 2018:
https://www.shreveporttimes.com/story/news/2015/07/23/lawyers-meet-with-potential-train-derailment-victims/30551793/

Moran Shipping, "Philadelphia Port Update *Athos I* Oil Spill," *Daily Port Update*, December 5, 2004. As of September 12, 2018:
http://phl.ports.moranshipping.com/Pages/Notices.aspx?NID=296&Month=December&Year=2004

———, "Philadelphia Update—Follow up *Athos I* Oil Spill," *Daily Port Update*, January 19, 2005. As of September 12, 2018:
http://phl.ports.moranshipping.com/Pages/Notices.aspx?NID=317&Month=January&Year=2005

Morris, J. D., "Federal Judge Overseeing PG&E's Probation Demands Answers on Camp Fire," *San Francisco Chronicle*, November 27, 2018. As of November 28, 2018:
https://www.sfchronicle.com/california-wildfires/article/Federal-judge-demands-answers-from-PG-E-over-Camp-13426313.php

Muldoon, Tony, "Tanker Spills Crude Oil in the Delaware River near Philadelphia After Hitting Cast-Iron Pipe," *Professional Mariner*, February 28, 2007. As of September 6, 2018:
http://www.professionalmariner.com/February-2007/Tanker-spills-crude-oil-in-the-Delaware-River-near-Philadelphia-after-hitting-cast-iron-pipe-0/

National Conference of Commissioners on Uniform State Laws, "Model Punitive Damages Act, 1996." As of October 28, 2018:
https://www.uniformlaws.org/HigherLogic/System/DownloadDocumentFile.ashx?DocumentFileKey=a2ebfda2-ab90-697b-8f11-641830a76357&forceDialog=0

National Transportation Safety Board, *Pipeline Accident Report: Pacific Gas and Electric Company Natural Gas Transmission Pipeline Rupture and Fire—San Bruno, California—September 9, 2010*, Report NTSB/PAR-11/01, September 26, 2011. As of August 23, 2018:
https://www.aga.org/sites/default/files/legacy-assets/our-issues/safety/pipleinesafety/Technicalreports/Documents/Final%20Report%20of%20NTSB%20San%20Bruno%20Accident%20Investigation.pdf

National Weather Service, *Tropical Weather Outlook, 2:00am Eastern Time*, August 13, 2017a. As of September 17, 2018:
https://www.nhc.noaa.gov/archive/xgtwo/gtwo_archive.php?basin=atl&fdays=5&current_issuance=201708130847

———, *Tropical Weather Outlook, 2:00pm Eastern Time*, August 17, 2017b. As of September 17, 2018:
https://www.nhc.noaa.gov/archive/xgtwo/gtwo_archive.php?current_issuance=201708172048&basin=atl&fdays=5

———, *Tropical Weather Outlook, 8:00pm Eastern Time*, August 19, 2017c. As of September 17, 2018:
https://www.nhc.noaa.gov/archive/xgtwo/gtwo_archive.php?current_issuance=201708200232&basin=atl&fdays=5

———, *Hurricane Harvey Tropical Cyclone Update,* August 24, 2017d. As of September 18, 2018:
https://www.nhc.noaa.gov/archive/2017/al09/al092017.update.08241656.shtml?

———, *Hurricane Harvey Advisory Number 18, 4:00pm Central Time*, August 24, 2017e. As of September 18, 2018:
https://www.nhc.noaa.gov/archive/2017/al09/al092017.public.018.shtml?

———, *Hurricane Harvey Advisory Number 23, 10:00pm Central Time*, August 25, 2017f. As of September 18, 2018:
https://www.nhc.noaa.gov/archive/2017/al09/al092017.public.018.shtml?

Nemec, Richard, "PG&E Fined $1.6B For San Bruno Pipeline Explosion," *Natural Gas Intelligence*, April 9, 2015. As of August 12, 2018:
https://www.naturalgasintel.com/articles/101930-pge-fined-16b-for-san-bruno-pipeline-explosion

Oberg, Ted, "Homeowners File Federal Lawsuit Against Arkema Plant in Crosby," *KTRK*, October 3, 2017. As of October 4, 2018:
https://abc13.com/homeowners-file-federal-lawsuit-against-arkema/2484965/

Ortiz, Alvaro, "Expert Says Chemical Industry Closely Following Upcoming Arkema Trial," *Houston Public Media*, October 22, 2018. As of November 20, 2018:
https://www.houstonpublicmedia.org/articles/shows/houston-matters/2018/10/22/308921/expert-says-chemical-industry-closely-following-upcoming-arkema-trial/

Pace, Nicholas M., and Lloyd Dixon, *Assigning Responsibility Following a Catastrophe: Alternatives to Relying Solely on Traditional Civil Litigation*, Santa Monica, Calif.: RAND Corporation, RR-1597-RC, 2017. As of September 6, 2019:
https://www.rand.org/pubs/research_reports/RR1597.html

Pacific Gas and Electric, "PG&E Continues Response Efforts at Scene of San Bruno Fire," press release, September 10, 2010a. As of June 6, 2018:
https://www.pge.com/about/newsroom/newsreleases/20100910/pge_continues_response_efforts_at_scene_of_san_bruno_fire.shtml

———, "PG&E Establishes 'Rebuild San Bruno Fund'—Uses Include Reimbursing City, Providing Residents Additional Immediate Financial Assistance," press release, September 13, 2010b. As of June 10, 2018:
https://www.pge.com/about/newsroom/newsreleases/20100913/pge_establishes_rebuild_san_bruno_fund.shtml

———, form letter to customers, October 21, 2010c. As of June 19, 2018:
https://www.pge.com/includes/docs/pdfs/myhome/customerservice/response/letter_to_customers.pdf

———, *San Bruno Approved Q&A*, October 19, 2010d. As of June 23, 2018: http://publicrecords.checksandbalancesproject.org/repository/20150130ReA1312012R/pdf/2010/10/SB_GT%26S_0010875.pdf

———, *Support for San Bruno January 20, 2012—DRAFT*, January 20, 2012. As of June 15, 2018:
ftp://ftp2.cpuc.ca.gov/PG&E20150130ResponseToA1312012Ruling/2012/02/SB_GT&S_0600637.pdf

———, *2015 Joint Annual Report to Shareholders*, 2016. As of September 21, 2018: http://s1.q4cdn.com/880135780/files/doc_financials/2015/2015-Annual-Report-Final.pdf

Pickoff-White, Lisa, David Marks, and Alex Emslie, "PG&E Gets $3M Fine for San Bruno Blast, Must Advertise Its Conviction on TV," *KQED*, January 26, 2017. As of September 4, 2018:
https://www.kqed.org/news/11287618/pge-gets-3m-fine-for-san-bruno-blast-must-advertise-its-conviction-on-tv

Public Law 85-256, An Act to Amend the Atomic Energy Act of 1954, as Amended, and for Other Purposes, September 2, 1957. As of August 20, 2019: https://www.govinfo.gov/content/pkg/STATUTE-71/pdf/STATUTE-71-Pg576.pdf

Public Law 91-604, Clean Air Amendments of 1970, December 31, 1970. As of August 20, 2019:
https://www.govinfo.gov/content/pkg/STATUTE-84/pdf/STATUTE-84-Pg1676.pdf

Public Law 92-500, Federal Water Pollution Control Act Amendments of 1972, October 18, 1972. As of August 20, 2019:
https://www.govinfo.gov/content/pkg/STATUTE-86/pdf/STATUTE-86-Pg816.pdf

Public Law 93-523, Safe Drinking Water Act, December 16, 1974. As of August 20, 2019:
https://www.govinfo.gov/content/pkg/STATUTE-88/pdf/STATUTE-88-Pg1660-2.pdf

Public Law 95-217, Clean Water Act of 1977, December 27, 1977. As of August 20, 2019:
https://www.govinfo.gov/content/pkg/STATUTE-91/pdf/STATUTE-91-Pg1566.pdf

Public Law 96-510, Comprehensive Environmental Response, Compensation, and Liability Act of 1980, December 11, 1980. As of August 20, 2019: https://www.govinfo.gov/content/pkg/STATUTE-94/pdf/STATUTE-94-Pg2767.pdf#page=22

Public Law 100-707, The Disaster Relief and Emergency Assistance Amendments of 1988, November 23, 1988. As of August 20, 2019:
https://www.hsdl.org/?abstract&did=806354

Public Law 101-380, Oil Pollution Act of 1990, August 18, 1990. As of August 20, 2019:
https://www.govinfo.gov/content/pkg/STATUTE-104/pdf/STATUTE-104-Pg484.pdf

Public Law 109-58, 119 Stat. 594, Energy Policy Act of 2005, August 8, 2005. As of October 24, 2019:
https://www.govinfo.gov/content/pkg/STATUTE-119/pdf/STATUTE-119-Pg594.pdf#page=418

Ramseur, Jonathan L., Oil Spills: Background and Governance, Washington, D.C.: Congressional Research Service, Report 7-5700, September 15, 2017. As of November 4, 2018:
https://fas.org/sgp/crs/misc/RL33705.pdf

Riddle, Amanda L., "PG&E San Bruno Explosion Cases," *The Docket*, San Mateo County Bar Association, 2016. As of September 2, 2018:
https://www.coreylaw.com/wp-content/uploads/2019/04/Centennial-Docket-PGE-Explosion-Article-Final.pdf

Rizer, Arthur L., III, "Lawyering Wars: Failing Leadership, Risk Aversion, and Lawyer Creep—Should We Expect More *Lone Survivors*?" *Indiana Law Journal*, Vol. 90, No. 3, Summer 2015, pp. 935–974.

San Mateo County Office of Emergency Services, *Post-San Bruno Fire Self-Evaluation*, 2012. As of August 3, 2018:
https://www.sanmateocourt.org/documents/grand_jury/2011/emergency_services.pdf

Silverfarb, Bill, "PG&E Hit by Five Lawsuits," *San Mateo Daily Journal*, October 20, 2010. As of July 9, 2018:
https://www.smdailyjournal.com/news/local/pg-e-hit-by-five-lawsuits/article_366b7973-4875-586d-a5e4-15ecb64bd394.html

Slaby, M. J., "Blount Well Water Found Contaminated," *Knoxville News Sentinel*, July 8, 2015. As of June 16, 2018:
https://www.questia.com/newspaper/1P2-38491514/blount-well-water-found-contaminated

Society of the Plastics Industry, Inc., *Safety and Handling of Organic Peroxides*, The Organic Peroxide Producers Safety Division, 2013. As of June 3, 2018:
http://www.plasticsindustry.org/sites/default/files/AS-109%20v%206%2021%20 2013.pdf

Soglin, Ari, "Help for Victims of San Bruno Fire," *Patch*, September 10, 2010. As of June 15, 2018:
https://patch.com/california/sanbruno/help-for-victims-of-san-bruno-fire

Spinelli, Dan, "A Year After an Environmental Disaster in Texas, Chemical Company Executives Face Charges," *Grist*, September 5, 2018. As of November 20, 2018:
https://grist.org/article/a-year-after-an-environmental-disaster-in-texas-chemical-company-executives-face-charges/

Stuckey, Alex, "Silent Spills—Part 2: For Crosby Residents, a 'Bitter Taste' About Arkema, and Little Help from Government," *Houston Chronicle*, 2018. As of October 3, 2018:
https://www.houstonchronicle.com/news/houston-texas/houston/article/For-Crosby-residents-a-bitter-taste-about-12771298.php

Terrazas, Alexis, "San Bruno Begins to Rebuild Nearly Eight Months After Pipeline Blast," *San Francisco Examiner*, May 7, 2011. As of July 23, 2018:
http://www.sfexaminer.com/san-bruno-begins-to-rebuild-nearly-eight-months-after-pipeline-blast/

Trevizo, Perla, "Arkema Hit with New Criminal Charges in 2017 Plant Fire During Harvey," *Houston Chronicle*, April 10, 2019. As of September 03, 2019:
https://www.chron.com/news/houston-texas/houston/article/Arkema-hit-with-new-criminal-charges-in-2017-fire-13756762.php

U.S. Chemical Safety and Hazard Investigation Board, *Organic Peroxide Decomposition, Release, and Fire at Arkema Crosby Following Hurricane Harvey Flooding—Crosby, Texas*, Report No. 2017-08-I-TX, May 2018. As of September 27, 2018:
https://www.csb.gov/file.aspx?DocumentId=6068

U.S. Coast Guard, *Investigation into the Striking of Submerged Objects by the Tank Vessel* Athos I *in the Delaware River on November 26, 2004 with a Major Discharge of Oil*, January 19, 2006. As of September 3, 2018:
https://www.dco.uscg.mil/Portals/9/DCO%20Documents/5p/CG-5PC/INV/docs/documents/AthosI.pdf

———, *Oil Pollution Act Liability Limits in 2017: Report to Congress*, August 21, 2018. As of November 2, 2018:
https://www.uscg.mil/Portals/0/NPFC/docs/PDFs/Reports//Liability_Limits_Report_2017.pdf

U.S. Commerce Department, "Remembering a Little Known Oil Spill with Out-Sized Impacts," news release, November 21, 2014. As of October 13, 2018:
http://www.professionalmariner.com/Web-Bulletin-2014/Remembering-a-little-known-oil-spill-with-out-sized-impacts/

U.S. Department of Transportation, Office of Railroad Safety Summary Report: Derailment and Subsequent Hazmat Release on CSX Transportation Freight Train # S541-01—Maryville, Tennessee—July 1, 2015, Federal Railroad Administration, 2017. As of September 24, 2019:
https://www.fra.dot.gov/eLib/details/L19078#p1_z5_gD_lAC_kMaryville

U.S. Environmental Protection Agency, *Interim Clean Water Act Settlement Penalty Policy*, March 1, 1995. As of October 6, 2018:
https://www.epa.gov/sites/production/files/documents/cwapol.pdf

U.S. Government Accountability Office, *U.S. Coast Guard National Pollution Funds Center: Improved Controls Needed for Oil Removal Disbursements and Action Needed for Sustainable Funding*, GAO-15-682, September 2015. As of August 31, 2018:
https://www.gao.gov/assets/680/672497.pdf

U.S. Sentencing Commission, "Sentencing Guidelines for United States Courts," *Federal Register*, Vol. 75, No. 13, January 21, 2010, pp. 3525–3539. As of August 20, 2019:
https://www.govinfo.gov/app/details/FR-2010-01-21/2010-970

———, *United States Sentencing Commission Guidelines Manual 2018*, Washington, D.C., effective November 1, 2018. As of August 20, 2019:
https://www.ussc.gov/guidelines/2018-guidelines-manual

Van Derbeken, Jaxon, "PG&E Admits Liability for San Bruno Pipeline Blast," *SFGate*, December 14, 2011. As of August 19, 2018:
https://www.sfgate.com/bayarea/article/PG-E-admits-liability-for-San-Bruno-pipeline-blast-2401186.php

———, "PG&E Settles More San Bruno Suits," *SFGate*, July 27, 2012. As of August 24, 2018:
https://www.sfgate.com/bayarea/article/PG-E-settles-more-San-Bruno-suits-3742194.php

Wade, Wes, "Alcoa Officers, Blount County Deputies Settle Lawsuits with CSX over Train Derailment," *Daily Times*, February 26, 2017. As of June 7, 2018:
https://www.thedailytimes.com/news/alcoa-officers-blount-county-deputies-settle-lawsuits-with-csx-over/article_fd660981-d8e8-5070-a3ac-1ab91f61a522.html

———, "CSX Facing Five More Lawsuits over Train Derailment, Including Wrongful Death of Blount County Firefighter," *Daily Times*, July 3, 2016. As of August 12, 2018:
https://www.thedailytimes.com/news/csx-facing-five-more-lawsuits-over-train-derailment-including-wrongful/article_765ecf71-6678-527b-b461-dd6647e300d0.html

———, "Jury Awards $13,213 in Damages in Blount County Train Derailment," *Daily Times*, March 8, 2018. As of August 15, 2018:
https://www.thedailytimes.com/news/jury-awards-in-damages-in-blount-county-train-derailment/article_8ab1a9fc-d791-52c7-a0ad-cb33d2e8a8b0.html

Waid, Raymond T., "Third Circuit Issues Long-Awaited Ruling in OPA Liability Case," *The Energy Law Blog*, April 5, 2018. As of November 2, 2018:
https://www.theenergylawblog.com/2018/04/articles/appellate/third-circuit-issues-long-awaited-ruling-in-opa-liability-case/

Whitfield, Stephanie, "Liberty County Files Million-Dollar Lawsuit Against Arkema Chemical Plant," *KHOU*, March 12, 2018. As of October 2, 2018: https://www.khou.com/article/news/local/liberty-county-files-million-dollar-lawsuit-against-arkema-chemical-plant/285-527837637

About the Authors

Lloyd Dixon is a senior economist at the RAND Corporation and Director of RAND's Center for Catastrophic Risk Management and Compensation. He has expertise in insurance, compensation, and liability issues. Dixon has examined the performance and regulation of various insurance and financial markets. He has examined the cost and affordability of flood insurance in New York City, and has written on residential and commercial wind insurance markets along the Gulf Coast. He recently completed a study of the impacts of changing wildfire risk on the homeowners insurance market for California's Fourth Climate Change Assessment and is currently examining the insurance practices of state and local governments as they relate to public buildings. Dixon has also examined compensation and liability policies in a number of different settings. Following the September 11 terrorist attacks, he described and assessed the complex web of insurance, charity, government, and tort payments that provided assistance to individuals and businesses harmed by the attacks. He is currently investigating the impact of compensation funds on post-disaster litigation. Dixon holds a B.S. in engineering and a B.A. in political science from Stanford University, and a Ph.D. in economics from the University of California at Berkeley.

Nicholas M. Pace is a senior social scientist at the RAND Corporation. His research focuses on how governmental entities, corporations, and other organizations, professions, and stakeholder groups operate within the context of the larger legal environment. Pace has a J.D.

CPSIA information can be obtained
at www.ICGtesting.com
Printed in the USA
LVHW081825230220
647925LV00010B/160

9 781977 403803